access to history

themes

RENAISSANCE ITALY

Robert Hole

Hodder & Stoughton

A MEMBER OF THE HODDER HEADLINE GROUP

Some other titles in the series:

Spain in the Reigns of Isabella and Ferdinand 1474–1516
Geoffrey Woodward   ISBN 0 340 68852 1

France: Renaissance, Religion and Recovery 1483-1610
Martyn Rady   ISBN 0 340 51804 9

Orders: please contact Bookpoint Ltd, 39 Milton Park, Abingdon, Oxon
OX14 4TD. Telephone: (44) 01235 400414, Fax: (44) 01235 400454. Lines
are open from 9.00 - 6.00, Monday to Saturday, with a 24 hour message
answering service. Email address: orders@bookpoint.co.uk

British Library Cataloguing in Publication Data
A catalogue for this title is available from the British Library

ISBN 0 340 70136 6

First published 1998

Impression number	10	9	8	7	6	5	4	3	2	1
Year			2002		2001		2000		1999	1998

The cover illustration is a self-portrait of Filippino Lippi, Uffizi, from AKG Photo,
London.
Illustrations by Ian Foulis & Associates Ltd, Saltash
Typeset by Sempringham publishing services, Bedford
Printed in Great Britain for Hodder & Stoughton Educational, a division of Hodder
Headline Plc, 338 Euston Road, London NW1 3BH by Redwood Books, Trowbridge,
Wiltshire

Contents

Preface

The original *Access to History* series was conceived as a collection of sets of books covering popular chronological periods in British history, such as 'The Tudors' and 'the nineteenth century', together with the histories of other countries, such as France, Germany, Russia and the USA. This arrangement complemented the way in which early-modern and modern history has traditionally been taught in sixth forms, colleges and universities. In recent years, however, other ways of dividing up the past have become increasingly popular. In particular, there has been a greater emphasis on studying relatively brief periods in considerable detail and on comparing similar historical phenomena in different countries. These developments have generated a demand for appropriate learning materials, and, in response, two new 'strands' are being added to the main series - *In Depth* and *Themes*. The new volumes build directly on the features that have made *Access to History* so popular.

To the general reader

Although *Access* books have been specifically designed to meet the needs of examination students, these volumes also have much to offer the general reader. *Access* authors are committed to the belief that good history must not only be accurate, up-to-date and scholarly, but also clearly and attractively written. The main body of the text (excluding the 'Study Guides') should, therefore, form a readable and engaging survey of a topic. Moreover, each author has aimed not merely to provide as clear an explanation as possible of what happened in the past but also to stimulate readers and to challenge them into thinking for themselves about the past and its significance. Thus, although no prior knowledge is expected from the reader, he or she is treated as an intelligent and thinking person throughout. The author tends to share ideas and explore possibilities, instead of delivering so-called 'historical truths' from on high.

To the student reader

It is intended that *Access* books should be used by students studying history at a higher level. Its volumes are all designed to be working texts, which should be reasonably clear on a first reading but which will benefit from re-reading and close study. To be an effective and successful student, you need to budget your time wisely. Hence you should think carefully about how important the material in a particular book is for you. If you simply need to acquire a general grasp of a topic, the following approach will probably be effective:

1. Read Chapter 1, which should give you an overview of the whole book, and think about its contents.

2. Skim through Chapter 2, paying particular attention to the opening section and to the headings and sub-headings. Decide if you need to read the whole chapter.
3. If you do, read the chapter, stopping at the end of every sub-division of the text to make notes.
4. Repeat stage 2 (and stage 3 where appropriate) for the other chapters.

If, however, your course - and your particular approach to it - demands a detailed knowledge of the contents of the book, you will need to be correspondingly more thorough. There is no perfect way of studying, and it is particularly worthwhile experimenting with different styles of note-making to find the one that best suits you. Nevertheless, the following plan of action is worth trying:

1. Read a whole chapter quickly, preferably at one sitting. Avoid the temptation - which may be very great - to make notes at this stage.
2. Study the flow diagram at the end of the chapter, ensuring that you understand the general 'shape' of what you have read.
3. Re-read the chapter more slowly, this time taking notes. You may well be amazed at how much more intelligible and straightforward the material seems on a second reading - and your notes will be correspondingly more useful to you when you have to write an essay or revise for an exam. In the long run, reading a chapter twice can, in fact, often save time. Be sure to make your notes in a clear, orderly fashion, and spread them out so that, if necessary, you can later add extra information.
4. Read the advice on essay questions, and do tackle the specimen titles. (Remember that if learning is to be effective, it must be active. No one - alas - has yet devised any substitute for real effort. It is up to you to make up your own mind on the key issues in any topic.)
5. Attempt the source-based questions. The guidance on tackling these exercises, which is generally given at least once in a book, is well worth reading and thinking about.

When you have finished the main chapters, go through the 'Further Reading' section. Remember that no single book can ever do more than introduce a topic, and it is to be hoped that - time permitting - you will want to read more widely. If *Access* books help you to discover just how diverse and fascinating the human past can be, the series will have succeeded in its aim - and you will experience that enthusiasm for the subject which, along with efficient learning, is the hallmark of all the best students.

Robert Pearce

1 Introduction: Renaissance Italy and European History

1 Ancient, Medieval, Renaissance and Modern

Renaissance Italy looked back to the past. That was then both the natural and the fashionable way to look. Present-day ideas of progress played no part in the mentality of the age. In many ways people embraced the new - for instance modern architecture was never more popular than in the Renaissance - but fundamentally people looked to the glories of the past. Imitation was regarded as a good thing. Italy had never been as great as it was in the days of the Roman Empire, or as noble as in the days of the Roman Republic, and it was the Ancient World that 'Renaissance Man' sought to emulate.

European history is sometimes divided into three main periods: Ancient (from the early Greeks in the eighth century BC, to the fall of the Roman Empire in the west in the fifth century AD), medieval (from the widespread adoption of Christianity in the fifth century to the Reformation in the sixteenth) and modern (from the sixteenth century to the present day). But these divisions are problematic and one of the main problems is where to fit in the Renaissance. To suggest that the Renaissance was 'the dawn of the modern world' is to miss the point altogether. Modern ways of thinking date from the scientific revolution of the seventeenth century, from men like Francis Bacon, Galileo and Isaac Newton, and are fundamentally different from the way Renaissance people thought. Modern thought is basically empirical - based on observation of the physical world and on practical experiments. Renaissance thought is based on tradition and authority; knowledge was sought not in the real world, but in books. Whereas the medieval world had looked chiefly to the authority of the Bible and the Christian theologians like St Thomas Aquinas, the Renaissance looked increasingly to the authority of the classical world; to Romans like Cicero and Greeks like Aristotle and Plato. But the Renaissance was not just a recreation of the Ancient World. People drew their inspiration from the Ancients, but created from them something new. Petrarch, a fourteenth-century Italian poet and one of the first Renaissance scholars, was one of many to use an old analogy: men took ideas from the Greeks and Romans just as bees take nectar from flowers. But from it they created honey, and Renaissance honey was quite distinctive from Ancient nectar.

Between the Ancient and Renaissance worlds lay the Middle Ages. Before the Roman Empire fell to the barbarian invasions of the fifth century AD, the Emperor Constantine was converted to Christianity and at least in theory and in name the late empire was a Christian one. The Roman Empire and medieval Christendom overlapped. In its last years the Roman Empire had two capitals and ultimately two emperors, one in the west at Rome and one in the east at Constantinople. From the year AD 476, at the insistence of the barbarians who were already supreme in Italy, there ceased to be a western emperor in Rome; an eastern emperor ruled in Constantinople until the fall of the city to the Turks in 1453. The Christian Church had split as early as the fourth century between the western, Latin, Catholic Church based on Rome and the eastern, Greek, Orthodox Church based on Constantinople. After there ceased to be a Roman emperor in the west, the vacuum was filled by the bishop of Rome, who took over from the Roman Empire the title of *Pontifex Maximus* - the chief priest or supreme pontiff.

Like the Middle Ages, the Renaissance was also a profoundly Christian age. Renaissance scholars and artists worked within a Christian context. Of course, the behaviour of most fell far below the high ideals of Christianity, but hardly any were atheists. These scholars were called humanists; the term humanism did not mean, as it has come to in the twentieth century, an ethical system independent of Christianity, but rather the study of the Greek and Latin classics. They continued to look to traditional authorities as the source of knowledge. Things were so 'because Aristotle said so'. The secret of knowledge was contained in books. The scientific revolution with its emphasis on empirical knowledge found by experiment and observation, and Galileo's and Newton's new understanding of the universe, belonged to a post-Renaissance, modern world, as far removed from the thinking of Renaissance humanists as those humanists were from the medieval schoolmen (or scholars). The Renaissance way of thinking, therefore, was distinct both from the medieval and from the modern, and we need to think in terms of four major periods of western European history rather than three - Ancient, Medieval, Renaissance and Modern. This notion was advanced by Denys Hay in a series of lectures in 1960 and the mass of work done since then has reinforced his argument.[1] If we are to understand the development of European thought over two millennia, the relationship between the Ancient and the modern worlds and the influence of Christianity upon European civilisation, then the Renaissance is a crucial area of study.

2 Italy: The Physical Environment

The Renaissance was a European phenomenon, but it began in Italy, the homeland of the Roman Empire, where the physical remains of the Ancient World - landscape, buildings, statues, coins and books - were abundantly present. The Italian peninsula was divided into a number of independent states whose boundaries changed over the period, but were centred on cities shown in the map on page 3.

In the north, the Alps is a range of high mountains, which cuts off Italy from Northern Europe, and which can be crossed only by a

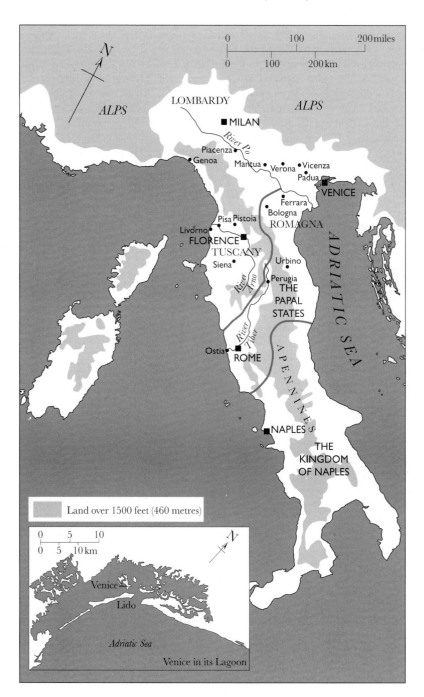

A map of Renaissance Italy

limited number of narrow mountain passes. Down the spine of Italy run the Apennines, a line of low hills only slightly higher than the Pennines in Northern England. The Apennines are far easier to cross than the Alps, but they still provide a natural boundary. Between the Alps and the Apennines, in the North Italian Plain, flows the River Po, an old river with a wide, flat valley. In the west of this valley, in a region called Lombardy, stands the city of Milan; in the extreme east is Venice. Milan controlled the most important Alpine passes and became the dominant power in this part of Italy. Between Milan and Venice were scattered a number of small, independent city states, like Padua, Mantua, Ferrara and Verona.

Venice, as all the world knows, has streets of water. It is built on an archipelago of islands in a lagoon at the head of the Adriatic Sea. Poised between land and sea, it was both a major Italian state and the centre of a great maritime empire which covered much of the Eastern Mediterranean. The wealth of the city came from its trade and it was on the maritime empire that the tradition and the pride of Venice rested. Venetian territory on the mainland of Italy - the *terraferma* - enjoyed nothing like the same prestige, but, in real terms, it became more and more important to the wealth and stability of the city. Before the Black Death in 1348, which killed between a third and a half of Italian city dwellers, Venice had a population of around 120,000; in 1420 it stood at about 84,000 and by 1509 had risen again to 115,000.

South of the Apennines, in the north-west, lies the region of Tuscany with Florence as its centre. Florence stands on the River Arno which joins the sea near Livorno - the port of Florence. Before it reaches the sea, however, the Arno flows through the city of Pisa. Florence was an important manufacturing centre and raw materials were transported to the city, and finished goods carried from the city, by water. Control of Pisa was crucial to the Florentine economy, but this proved difficult to maintain - a perennial thorn in the side. To the south of Florence, on the other side of Chianti country, stands the city of Siena; a smaller rival, fiercely independent, she prevented Florentine expansion southward. Before the Black Death, Florence had a population of around 90,000; in 1427 it was perhaps as low as 40,000, but by 1500 it had risen to 80,000.

The Papal States ran like a sash across the middle of the peninsula from south-west to north-east. They comprised a number of small states, technically under papal jurisdiction, but ruled in fact by virtually independent vicars. The term 'vicar' means simply a substitute; in church parishes the original 'vicar' was a substitute for a rector. The vicars who ruled the papal states in place of the pope were not clergymen but secular rulers, some of whom were marquises or dukes. These states varied in character, partly dependent on their proximity to Rome. The area immediately around the city was known as the Patrimony of St Peter and, although it contained the castles of powerful and independent Roman barons, it was on the whole more closely under the papal eye than remote cities high in the Apennines or beyond them, like Urbino and Bologna. The city of Rome itself has been described as an appendage of the papal court.[2] Sited on the River Tiber about 17 miles from the sea at Ostia, Rome was not only the Ancient western capital of the Empire, but also the home of the papacy. The basilica of St Peter and St Paul was the mother church of western Christendom, where lay the bones of the Apostle Peter, the first Pope. Adjoining the church was the Vatican Palace where the successors of St Peter, the popes, lived from 1377 onwards. Without the papacy Rome was nothing; in 1420 when the papacy returned after a long absence it had perhaps as few as 25,000 inhabitants, and in 1526 it still had a population of only 54,000 - about half the size of Florence and Venice.

All of the Italian mainland south of the Papal States was the Kingdom of Naples. This was by far the most remote and backward part of the peninsula. The city of Naples, set in its spectacular bay in sight of Vesuvius, was one of the great cities of Europe, an important home of art and learning, but the only significant urban centre south of Rome. And that is what Renaissance Italy was really about - urban centres. The Renaissance was fundamentally an urban phenomenon which hardly touched the countryside. Perhaps that is why it started in Italy. France and England were still essentially feudal, landed, rural societies. Wealth in Italy depended less on land and more on trade, commerce and manufacture in the large number of cities in north and central Italy. The Renaissance was a capitalist not a feudal phenomenon. The money which paid for it - in other words the wealth of the patrons who employed the artists and scholars - came largely from capitalist business concerns which were urban based. That money lay at the heart of the cultural movement we call the Renaissance.

3 Renaissance and Re-birth: Definitions

Why do we call it the 'Renaissance'? This is, after all a French term for an Italian movement, which has been regularly used only since the middle of the nineteenth century - though the art historian Giorgio Vasari had used an equivalent Italian word *Rinàscita* in 1550. The word Renaissance means, of course, 're-birth', and it combines looking back to the Ancient World with that sense of newness which birth brings.

One of the things the word Renaissance now means is a period in history, but there is little general agreement about which dates to assign to it. In the History of Art, the decade of the 1420s, when the painter Masaccio, the sculptor Donatello and the architect Brunelleschi were all working in Florence, is frequently described as a time of 'breakthrough'. But most art historians would want to regard

Giotto (1266/7-1337) as an early Renaissance painter, and students of humanist scholarship would include Petrarch (1304-74), the poet, and Boccaccio (1313-75), the short story writer, as early Renaissance scholars. Boccaccio's *Decameron* is set in the year of the great plague, 1348, and has been described as being a medieval, pre-Renaissance work, but one which also reflects 'the decline of the feudal aristocracy and the ever-increasing vitality of the bourgeoisie, especially in the spheres of banking and commerce' so characteristic of the Renaissance.[3] Boccaccio's activities in searching out early manuscripts of ancient writers in the monastic library at Monte Cassino clearly identifies him as a Renaissance humanist scholar. All this suggests that society in the second quarter of the fourteenth century, although still fundamentally medieval, was already marked with unmistakable signs of an emerging Renaissance. The 1490s is often seen as the beginning of the High Renaissance which saw not only Raphael, Leonardo and Michelangelo at the height of their powers, but also witnessed the trauma of the French invasion of Italy in 1494. For many purposes, the Sack of Rome by the armies of the Holy Roman Emperor in 1527, followed by the restoration of the Pope to Rome in 1530, can mark the end of the Renaissance, but not until Michelangelo's death in 1564 can we really abandon the term. The fifteenth century, often referred to by its Italian name of the *Quattrocento*, and the first few decades of the sixteenth century comprised the heart of the Renaissance in Italy. So, whilst acknowledging that the Italian Renaissance can be dated from the second quarter of the fourteenth century to the third quarter of the sixteenth, most of this book will focus on the period from 1380 to 1530, and much from 1420 to 1513.

But, with all its complexity and controversy, can the word 'Renaissance' be defined more precisely than as just a period in history? The Oxford English Dictionary offers us 'the great revival of art and letters, under the influence of classical models, which began in Italy in the fourteenth century and continued during the fifteenth and sixteenth'. Certainly that is central, but there is more to it, as the Victorian historian Walter Pater saw in 1871: 'The word *Renaissance* indeed is now generally used to denote ... a whole complex movement of which that revival of classical antiquity was but one element or symptom.'[4] Certainly a new stress on the individual human being can be discerned. This is very much a world in which humanity is at the centre. No finished painting of the Italian Renaissance is a still life or a landscape; the principal feature of all paintings is humankind, men and women. The Greek word for man is *anthropos*, and the Renaissance can properly be described as being, in its essence, anthropocentric - 'centred on humanity'.

But this is not the right place for an historian to try to define the term 'Renaissance'. Historians should examine the evidence first and then draw conclusions afterwards, so a full definition will not be attempted until the final chapter of this book.

4 Burckhardt and Beyond

> M.chll?

The term 'Renaissance' had been in use for less than a generation
when Jacob Burckhardt explored the concept in a seminal book, *The
Civilization of the Renaissance in Italy*, first published in 1860. This established the concept of Renaissance Man as an individualist with hints
of universality and paganism: in John Hale's words, it suggested 'man
had escaped from the medieval thought-dungeon and the world, with
its expanding physical and mental horizons, became his oyster.'[5] Most
aspects of Burckhardt's definition have been criticised, with much
justice; Burckhardt created a model which later historians have
largely demolished. Yet often what is being criticised is the impression
his book gives rather than its precise words. If you go back to
Burckhardt you will find that he is often more cautious, more subtle,
more judicious than many criticisms of him imply, but there is a
general thrust to his argument which can no longer be accepted. If
Renaissance History were an oyster, then Burckhardt would be the
grit, not the pearl.

He described the Middle Ages as a time when human conscious-
ness 'lay dreaming or half awake beneath a common veil ... of faith,
illusion, and childish prepossession'.[6] He was a Protestant with little
natural sympathy for the medieval Church and its scholars. The
Renaissance, he implied, was a dramatic break with the past, a new
age in which man as an individual emerged - cosmopolitan, slightly
pagan, with the all-sided ability of the universal man, *l'uomo universale*. In fact, later work has transformed our view of the Middle Ages;
now it appears as rich and culturally diverse, a time of immense intellectual and artistic achievement. The Renaissance can be seen as
emerging gradually from this complex civilisation and the lines of
continuity between the Middle Ages and the Renaissance need as
much attention as the differences. Nor did Renaissance man have a
whiff of paganism about him. Paintings of the Virgin Mary far
outnumbered those of Venus. Almost everyone in Renaissance Italy
believed in the Christian faith; their interest in the Ancient World
did not mean they flirted with its religion. And as for the universal
man, when young people today read Leon Battista Alberti's description of himself, written around 1460, which Burckhardt cited as
evidence of universality, they laugh at his foolish pretension as he
claims to have been quite brilliant at everything.[7] Leonardo da Vinci
was a supremely talented artist who completed very few paintings
because he was diverted by other pursuits in which he was less accom-
plished, such as designing impractical inventions. It would be unfair
to say that he was less the universal man than a skilful Jack-of-all-
trades who neglected the one in which he was a master, but like many
caricatures, this has a grain of truth in it.

Burckhardt placed a great emphasis on the role of the humanist
writers whose revival of Latin and Greek scholarship lay at the heart of

the Renaissance. In the 20 years after the Second World War, Paul Oscar Kristeller, Eugenio Garin and Hans Baron studied the nature of humanism which each interpreted in a quite different way. The last 40 years of the twentieth century saw less emphasis being placed on humanism and more on social history. The work of scholars like Guido Ruggiero, Lauro Martines and Richard Trexler shone light on themes like the role of women, on violence, sexuality, and the importance of ritual and ceremony. Much attention was paid to individual cities, their political life and constitutions and the relation of these to their social and economic arrangements. The 'Myth of Venice' was deconstructed and the power of the Medici in Florence reassessed in light of the difficulties they faced in controlling a city with a powerful republican tradition. Both the Church and the mercenaries were shown to be better than they had been painted. In the world of the visual arts, the economic context in which painters, sculptors and architects worked was closely examined and the influence of both patrons and market forces on individual works demonstrated.[8] So, as well as considering the work of the humanists, this book will explore the other developments mentioned in this paragraph. It will not concern itself too much with the historiographical debates of the past, but will try to paint a picture of Renaissance Italy as scholars understand it today.

References

1   Published as D. Hay, *The Italian Renaissance in its historical background* (Cambridge University Press, 1961).
2   P. Partner, *Renaissance Rome 1500-1559: a portrait of a society* (University of California Press, 1977), p. 56.
3   G.H. McWilliam, 'Translator's Introduction' to Boccaccio, *The Decameron* Second Edition (Penguin Books, 1995), p. lxxxiii.
4   W. Pater, *The Renaissance* [1873] (Fontana, 1961), p. 33.
5   J.R. Hale, *Encyclopaedia of the Italian Renaissance* (Thames and Hudson, 1981), p. 279.
6   J. Burckhardt, *The Civilization of the Renaissance in Italy* [1860] (Penguin Books, 1990), p. 98.
7   This is easily available in *The Portable Renaissance Reader* (Penguin, 1977), pp. 480-92. Compare Burckhardt, pp. 102-3.
8   In the note on further reading on pp. 134-5, see Hale and Brucker on Florence; Chambers and Pullan on Venice; Partner on Rome; Hay on the church; Mallett on the mercenaries; Baxendall and Thomas on painting.

Making notes on 'Renaissance Italy'

If you are to understand the rest of this book, it is important that you read this chapter carefully. However, you may not need to make detailed notes on it, at least not at this stage. You will be advised to re-read parts of it at later points and all of it when you have finished the whole book, and it may be useful to take notes then. The places shown on the map are mentioned throughout the book and it is vital that you know their geographical position.

How you decide to use this book will depend to a great extent on what you are studying. If you are following a wide-ranging course on European History in the Age of the Renaissance and the Reformation, then Renaissance Italy will form only a part of it, and you may not need to answer the detailed essay questions at the end of each chapter. The selection of wider and more general questions at the end of Chapter nine may be more appropriate for you. To answer them you will need to read all of this book, but may not need to make full notes on all of it.

If, however, you are following a specialised course on Renaissance Italy or on The Renaissance then you will need detailed notes on each of the following chapters and should attempt to answer the essay questions which follow most of them. In that case, you should try to read some other books which deal with the subject matter of each chapter in more detail. Appropriate books for this purpose are listed in the section on further reading on pages 134-5. Remember you are reading these other books for two purposes: firstly, to get additional information; secondly, to get a variety of interpretations, alternative arguments and a different point of view. When you have got hold of a suitable book, you do not need to read it from cover to cover: use this book to identify the main themes, places or people you need to know more about, then look these up in the table of contents and the index of the other book(s). It may be that only, say, 20 pages of that book will be relevant to the question you are investigating, so it is worth spending a little time to discover which parts of it merit reading. If you already know quite a lot about the topic and have a basic set of notes from this book, you can often extract what you need from another book in a couple of hours or so. If you have tracked the other book down in your local library, it is a good idea to work on it there rather than borrowing it. The disciplined atmosphere of a quiet library should help you to use the book quickly and efficiently. Those who claim they 'can't work in libraries' should learn to - or give up being a student.

2 Making Money: The Economic Framework

Culture costs money. Scholars and artists needed rich patrons. The Renaissance happened in Florence, Venice and Rome because there were wealthy men and women there who had disposable income which they could spend on learning and the arts. As fifteenth-century Italians would have been the first to acknowledge, any study of the Renaissance in Italy must start with the wealth which made it possible. How did the rich of Florence, Venice, Rome and elsewhere make their money?

Rome was a special case. There the only major source of income was the Church, but, as Rome was the home of the papacy and of the central administrative structure of western Christendom, that source was a massive one. The amount of money sent by churches from all over Europe to the papacy has been much exaggerated but was still considerable and the vast bulk of it came to Rome. Without the papacy, Rome would have been a minor town with no significant trade, commerce or manufacture. The economy, which allowed it to become one of the major centres of Renaissance art and learning, was unique. Elsewhere, the main sources of income came from capitalist businesses, from the profits of trade and commerce, of banking and of the manufacture of goods - mostly but not entirely textiles. The most important manufacturing centre was Florence and the main trading centre Venice, but both activities were widespread.

1 Trade and Commerce: The City of Venice

Venice was not the only trading nation in Renaissance Italy, but it was by far the most important. Venetian trade pre-dated the Renaissance; the best known of all Venetians, Marco Polo, traded with India and China in the 1290s. Trade lay at the heart of the Venetian empire; as David Chambers points out, 'the most vital organs of the empire were, therefore, warehouses, ships' holds, barges and pack-horses'.[1] The Venetian maritime empire was an informal empire of trade. Venice did not govern colonies, but protected its trade routes. War galleys on sea and armed garrisons on land prevented other nations encroaching on profitable commercial activities. These trade routes stretched down the Adriatic coast, then went in all directions, but principally through the Greek islands to Egypt and the Orient, to Constantinople and the Black Sea ports. You can still see the remains of Venetian forts on many Greek islands today. Venetian ships brought timber, grain and salt, fruit and cheap wine from the Mediterranean as well as the more exotic goods of the East - spices and silk, cotton, drugs and jewels. Goods from all over the empire were stored in city warehouses before being re-exported to the rest of Europe. At the end of the fifteenth century, the Portuguese discovery of a sea route to India caused a degree of panic but did not significantly affect Venice's trade with the East. In 1502 a special advisory board on the spice trade was set up, 'to provide remedies lest the King of Portugal takes the silver and gold out of our hands to the manifest ruin of our business affairs and posterity'.[2] But a more serious threat was the expansion of the Ottoman Empire, from around 1414. The Venetians resisted them at Gallipoli in 1416, but by 1430 the Turks were making significant gains on the Greek mainland. This culminated in the capture of Constantinople in 1453 and a Turkish advance through the Balkans towards Vienna in the 1460s and 1470s. However, Venetian trade proved remarkably resilient and the island of Cyprus was added to the empire in 1489. Venetian traders managed to co-exist remarkably well with the Turkish invaders in the eastern Mediterranean. The city's economic interest dictated that they did not behave in a provocative way. Venice continued to prosper.

Venice showed little interest in the *terraferma* before the fifteenth century. The city was wedded to the sea (the Doge - Duke - of Venice symbolically threw a ring into the Adriatic on Ascension Day each year) and the Italian mainland was largely neglected. But Venetian goods also travelled overland, through the Alpine passes into Austria and Germany and these routes needed protection too. The expansion of the Milanese Empire under Giangaleazzo Visconti posed a threat and following his death in 1402 the Venetian *terraferma* began to grow (see pages 43, and 71). Cities like Vicenza, Verona and Padua came under Venetian rule, and for the first half of the fifteenth century Venice and Milan struggled with each other to be the dominant power in the North Italian Plain.

Boat and shipbuilding were crucial industries in the city. As well as a large number of minor boatbuilding yards where a wide variety of small craft were made for use in the city and further afield, Venice also possessed the largest industrial complex in the western world - a state shipbuilding yard called the Arsenal where war galleys were constructed. By the sixteenth century, the Arsenal covered 60 acres (the equivalent area of about 40 football pitches) and employed around two thousand men.[3] Workers there, *Arsenalotti* as they were known, were highly prised if not highly paid; their kudos was not matched by their wages. The ships they built had developed directly from the galleys of the Ancient World and combined oar-power with sails. Criminals were regularly assigned to be oarsmen in the galleys. War galleys accompanied convoys of merchant ships carrying goods to the city.

The most important citizens of Venice, the patricians were intimately connected with trade (see page 39). In old feudal societies, like England and France, it was land-holding that was prestigious; commercial life was considered somewhat vulgar. This was far from the case in Renaissance Italy. Just as in Florence the leading citizens were involved in cloth manufacture and banking, so in Venice the patricians were deeply immersed in commercial life. They were capitalists who invested the profits of trade back into the business. They managed the galley convoys, they acted as governors of important trading posts in the empire, they controlled the warehouses, customs offices and courts which regulated trade. In short, they had a firm grip on the heart of the commercial life of the city and the empire. The wealth of the city of Venice came from trade, but that wealth went essentially to the richest of its private citizens, not to the state. Certainly customs duties, and various taxes on imports and exports made a significant contribution to the public coffers, but the major tax was the *decima*, a direct tax of a tenth on the value of real property (i.e. immovable property like land and houses). There was also a range of indirect taxes and some dependence on public loans, from private citizens to the state, which played an important role in raising funds rapidly in times of need. Trade made Venetians rich and gave them employment. True, this allowed them to contribute to public finances, but it was their private wealth that was most significant. These individual fortunes financed much of the scholarly and artistic activity of the Renaissance.

As in other Italian cities, the Jews played an important part in the economy of Venice. Many small businesses needed to be able to borrow sums of money, but Christian bankers were prevented from making loans at fixed interest rates by the laws against usury. These were based on Christ's injunction in the Sermon on the Mount that people should make loans freely and not hope for gain from them. Moses's teaching had been less restrictive and allowed Jews to engage in financial transactions forbidden to Christians.[4] Because such dealings were crucial to the well-being of the economy, the Venetian authorities allowed the Jews to live and work in the city. Yet there was a great deal of prejudice against them. They were blamed for killing Christ and it was popularly (but quite erroneously) believed that, at Easter, Jews would kidnap Christian boys and crucify them in re-enactment of the crucifixion of Christ. This prejudice against the Jews, together with the economic need for their services, caused the pendulum to swing to and fro. At one time they would be given privileges to trade in the city, then those privileges would be withdrawn, and later re-granted. It was astute of Shakespeare to set his story of Shylock amongst the merchants of Venice. In March 1516 all Jews in the city were required to live in the New Foundry, a disused iron works built like a fortress with a single entrance, where they could be confined at night. The Italian for foundry is *ghetto* and so Venice gave another new word to the world.

2 Manufacturing and Banking: The City of Florence

At the heart of the commercial centre of Florence, only the width of a narrow street away from the Guildhall of the powerful *Arte della Lana* (the Wool Guild), stands the city church of *Orsanmichele*. Dominating the exterior of this church, on all four sides, are 14 large niches, containing life-size statues of the saints in bronze or marble. Three of these are shown in the illustration on page 27. Each niche was adopted by one of the city's guilds and each guild commissioned a major sculptor to create a figure sufficiently magnificent to bring them glory. The guilds dominated the city politically and economically. Guilds were associations of employers not workers, of masters not men. Their members constituted the urban élite. It was guild membership which provided the entrance to political life (see page 46). This was dominated by the seven major guilds: the cloth importers, judges and notaries, bankers, furriers, doctors and pharmacists, silk manufacturers and the wool guild. But there were 14 minor guilds as well and other niches of *Orsanmichele* were filled by statues commissioned by the guilds of the butchers, tanners, armourers, smiths, drapers, masons and carpenters.

Probably over 60 per cent of the Florentine poor worked in trades which were regulated by guilds. That regulation could be fierce. It controlled entry to the guild, and anyone who was not a member could not practise their trade in the city. It enforced a quality control over the goods produced to maintain the reputation of the city for the highest quality in the markets of the world. Guilds also regulated their workers. The consuls who administered the guild employed 'messengers' who acted as bailiffs, strong-armed men well able to intimidate people. These would take the goods of those workers who were in debt to, or in dispute with, their employers; the guild was a power in the city and these matters were settled without reference to those who administered justice in Florence. Troublesome workers were 'blacklisted' and other guild members told not to employ them.

The *Lana* (Wool) Guild was overwhelmingly the most powerful. The manufacture of woollen cloth employed at times perhaps 30,000 men and women, over one third of the city's population, and it was for its manufacture of cloth that Florence was famed throughout Europe. There were about 200 firms headed by (usually) two capitalist businessmen who often took great risks with their investments. The older practice of having a 'sleeping' partner who invested the money and a working partner who conducted the business, became largely replaced by two equal partners, both of whom invested their money and engaged in the work. They would buy wool from all over Europe (some came from as far afield as England) and shipped it to Florence, making the last stage of the journey up the River Arno. Here they usually had a workshop where the raw wool was prepared for spinning. It was then carried through the city streets to the homes of the women who spun it into thread. Brokers took the spun wool to weavers whose looms were either in their homes or in small workshops. The cloth was then taken on to fullers and dyers for finishing. The poorest of these workers were paid a pittance; their employers were some of the richest businessmen in Europe. The finished cloth was exported from Florence to the rest of Christendom, and none had a finer reputation. So it was a shock when, in 1425, two statues in niches of *Orsanmichele* commissioned by other guilds were perceived to

> surpass in beauty and ornamentation that of the *Lana* guild. So it may truly be said that this does not redound to the honour of the *Lana* guild, particularly when one considers the magnificence of that guild which has always sought to be the master and the superior of the other guilds.[5]

Steps were immediately taken to put this right and a bronze statue of St Stephen, the patron saint of the Wool Guild, was commissioned from Ghiberti, one of the leading sculptors of the day, who had been responsible for the statues in the two 'superior' niches.

One of the guilds whose niche had temporarily outshone that of the *Arte della Lana* was the *Cambio*, the association of the bankers. Bankers were less numerous - there were about 80 firms - and employed far fewer workers. They were less visible, but they contributed as significantly to the wealth and the economic reputation of Florence. Florence was the banking capital of Europe. Florentines stood at the cutting edge of new economic practices; they were innovators who were in the process of creating the new commercial procedures and financial services needed by a capitalist economy. Under a feudal, rural, agricultural economy, few communities were genuinely self-sufficient, though many came close to it. Even within a village there was some specialisation and division of labour. But virtually everyone produced goods of some kind or another - food, clothing, machinery and tools and so on; unlike the cities they were not involved in service industries. In the capitalist, urban and international economy which Renaissance Italy initiated, trade and commerce became far more complex and sophisticated. Instead of keeping accounts in their heads, businessmen invested time and effort in maintaining quite elaborate records. They invented the system of double-entry book-keeping which a leading twentieth-century economist regarded as 'the towering monument' of capitalist practice which turned 'the unit of money into a tool of rational cost-profit calculations'.[6] This system set out income and expenditure clearly in parallel credit and debit columns. So important did money become as the unit of exchange, that some people engaged wholly, not in the production of goods, but in the manipulation of money and credit. Those men were the bankers.

There were two kinds of banks which served quite distinct functions. On the one hand were the small banks, the *banchi a minuto*, which met the everyday needs of the small traders of the city. On the other hand were the international banks which had branches throughout Italy and all over Europe from Spain to Constantinople, from England to Jerusalem. These provided the international merchants with Letters of Credit and Bills of Exchange which could be converted into cash at other branches throughout Europe; they arranged loans and they collected debts. The Florentine bankers to the papacy acted virtually as tax-farmers. Normally each branch of an international bank was technically independent; although in fact part of the same business, they were legally separate and so not responsible for each others' debts and liabilities. One of the main problems which both international banks and small banks faced was the canon law of usury (see page 12). As Christian businesses they were unable to charge a fixed-rate of interest on loans, though investments which involved a degree of risk were permitted. Their double-entry account books avoided using the word 'interest'; loans were disguised as gifts which were repaid by a slightly larger gift. The exchange of money from one currency to another also permitted a profit and often this procedure was used to conceal the payment of interest. It was widely understood that bankers inevitably broke this Church law and were likely to have something on their conscience. As they approached death and judgement, many would make gifts to the Church, found libraries, build chapels, anything to ease their route to Heaven. The sycophantic bookseller, Vespasiano di Bisticci, even suggested that his patron Cosimo de' Medici, the greatest Florentine banker of his day,

| had prickings of conscience that certain portions of his wealth - where it came from I cannot say - had not been righteously gained, and to remove this weight from his shoulders he held conference with Pope Eugenius as to the load which lay on his conscience. Pope Eugenius
5 remarked to Cosimo that, if he was bent on unburdening his soul, he might build a monastery.[7]

Cosimo spent a small fortune of 40,000 florins re-building the Monastery of S. Marco, and establishing there the origins of one of the great libraries of Renaissance Italy. Whether inspired by guilt or by a genuine spirit of patronage, it was the profits of manufacture and commerce which paid for the Florentine Renaissance.

3 The Risks and Pleasures of Making Money

We must not let these prickings of Cosimo's conscience mislead us. Renaissance people loved making money. It was a constant source of delight to them. There was nothing safe about the early days of capitalist enterprise. Great fortunes could be won and lost; great risks had to be taken and those men who took those risks were seen as *heroic*. This same word was applied to a fresco painter like Michelangelo who covered a wall with wet plaster and created his picture in the ten hours it took that plaster to dry. The challenge which faced an international merchant called for no less heroism. The vitality and vigour one can see in the fresco self portrait of Filippino Lippi on the cover of this book, with its lively brushstrokes, reflects the energy and enthusiasm with which merchants pursued profit.

In his diary, the Florentine merchant Gregorio Dati recalled how he started business in debt, but recouped his fortunes by marriage, putting the dowry his wife brought him into the business (see page 28). Soon he lost both wife and money. Then,

> 1 due to the bad debt that Giovanni Stefani contracted with our company, I found myself rather short of money. In 1393, I married my second wife. The dowry was substantial but I spent too much. In 1394 I was captured and robbed at sea and suffered considerable losses. I went into partner-
> 5 ship with Michele (di Ser Parenti) in 1396 and I did very well up to the year 1402. When I parted company with Michele, I had about 1,000 florins. I went into partnership with Piero Lana and engaged myself to invest 2,000 florins. At this point fortune turned against me.[8]

Similar complaints were heard from sixteenth-century Venice. Zuare Zane complained his family firm had lost money by fire in the city and losses at sea, as well as having to meet the high costs of dowries for three daughters. In 1524 a ship carried 1,300 butts of wine to England and on the way back was captured by a Frenchman; Zuare's brother was taken prisoner.

> 1 Upon that ship were our wools, kerseys [woollen cloths], cloths and tin, and a large sum in cash to buy salt at Ibiza. The loss amounted to over 22,000 ducats. We say nothing of the cargo of sugar we were due to take on in Cádiz and the profit expected from the merchandise and from
> 5 various freight charges of more than 8,000 ducats, and there was a clear loss of another 11,000 ducats and more - a thing one shudders even to hear about because at that time we were debtors on Rialto for more than 7,000 ducats.[9]

Neither Florentine manufacturers nor Venetian merchants were particularly highly taxed, but both complained bitterly. Especially in the early Renaissance, the rich avoided conspicuous consumption in case this led to their tax bills rising. The Florentine merchant Giovanni Morelli epitomised this attitude in the advice he left to his sons:

> 1 Don't advertise the fact that you are rich. Instead do the contrary. If you are worth 10,000 florins, you should maintain a standard of living as though you possessed 5,000. You should demonstrate this in your speech, the clothes which you and your family wear, your food, your ser-
> 5 vants and your horses. And don't reveal your true worth to anyone: neither relatives, nor friends nor partners. Don't reveal your wealth by lav-

ish possessions, but buy only what you need for your subsistence. You should always complain about your taxes: say that your assessment should be halved, that you have large debts and heavy expenses, that you
10 must pay the obligations in your father's will, that you have incurred business losses, that the harvest from your farms is poor, that you will have to buy grain, wine, wood and other staples. Don't make these statements so wild you will be ridiculed, but tell lies which are close to the
15 truth, so you will be believed and not considered a liar. And this is quite legitimate, because you are not lying to steal from another, but rather so that your property will not be taken from you unjustly.[10]

One feels that all this complaining was really part of the fun of being rich. Generosity to one's family and to deserving charities was encouraged, but only within the limits one could afford. The Florentine Giovanni Rucellai, around 1460, advised his sons:

1 One must know how to spend money and to acquire possessions. He who spends only in eating and dressing, or who does not know how to disburse money for the benefit and honour of his family, is certainly not wise. Of necessity, the rich man must be generous, for generosity is the
5 most noble virtue that he can possess, and to exercise it requires wisdom and moderation. But who gives beyond his means soon dissipates his fortune.[11]

Making money was not only pleasurable, it also brought prestige to those of the highest social status. In feudal societies, such as Aragon, commerce was seen as vulgar; not so in Italy, as a Spanish Ambassador, Don Alonso della Cueva, noted in Venice:

they are not forbidden to engage in commerce, nor is it thought unseemly for them to do so, although being rulers and not subjects, they might well be ashamed of it. On the contrary, such activity adds to their reputation, and does not diminish it.[12]

Girolamo Priuli, who belonged to a leading patrician family in Venice, observing that 'business is a good thing for the public economy', noted in his diary, 'My father, proud of his native country and its liberty, did not spare himself day or night in finding ways of making money.'[13]

4 The Cities and the Countryside

A note of caution is necessary. This picture of the Italian economy has concentrated almost exclusively on the major urban centres of wealth and culture. Indeed, we could argue that 'the Renaissance' affected only those rich towns. Most people lived in villages and hamlets, scattered in a countryside which Renaissance learning and art never touched. They never enjoyed the fabulous wealth of the élite, never depended on trade and manufacture for their livelihood. The age-old cultivation of the soil, a relatively high degree of self-sufficiency and the bare minimum necessary to support life characterised the personal economies of most Italians in this period. Historians are rightly cautious - sometimes even embarrassed - about concentrating on a rich élite. At one time it was assumed that the poor could be ignored as they didn't matter, although recently there has been, quite properly, a real attempt to recover and re-create their lives. But often the concentration on the wealthy is forced on historians by the availability of written evidence. The educated, articulate rich wrote about their lives and feelings in a way that the poor were rarely able to. Too often we see the poor only through the eyes of the rich when they appear in court or as suppliants for charity.

The problem is, however, more fundamental than this for the student of the Renaissance. The Renaissance was an élite movement. The most eminent of the scholars and artists lived lives of relative privilege and depended on the patronage of the rich. Peasants toiling in the fields did not read Cicero and Plato and never had an opportunity to see paintings by Raphael or sculptures by Michelangelo. But neither did the money which paid those artists and scholars come from the labour of the rural poor. It was largely the profits of urban trade and industry which paid for the books and the buildings, the paintings and sculptures which characterised the Renaissance. Whilst we must never forget the many who worked the fields of rural Italy, it is on the few urban money-makers we must concentrate if we want to explain why the Renaissance happened in the cities of Italy.

5 Conclusion

In our analysis of Renaissance Italy we deal with the economic framework first. Why? Some historians might say, because you have to begin somewhere and, since everything relates to everything else, it does not really matter where you start. Marxist historians, on the other hand, would argue that the economic base of society determines the social and political structure, culture and ideology which grows out of it. But you do not have to accept the Marxist belief that the type of economy (Marx called it the 'mode of production') predetermines all else, to recognise that the economic practices of early capitalism did result in the growth of busy cities with wealthy citizens who had money to spend on luxuries. In this chapter we have identified three major economic activities which were important in the development of capitalism - trade, manufacturing and banking. The patricians of Venice invested money in trade and made a profit from it which they ploughed back into their businesses; in Florence, textile manufacturers and bankers did the same. Rome was a unique exception; money flowed into the city, not because of capitalist enterprise, but because it was the administrative centre of the Church. Marx talked about the transition from one mode of production (feudalism) to

another (capitalism) and, again, one does not have to accept his asser-
tion that certain results would inevitably follow, to notice some
dramatic differences between the two economic systems. Feudalism
depended largely on agriculture and established a rural society in
which profits came from renting farms and passed to an aristocratic
landed class. Capitalism was urban; under it cities thrived and profits
went to those who were willing to invest money and take risks.
Whether the city was a great trading centre like Venice, or engaged in
textile manufacture or financial services, like Florence, the result was
the same - a sizeable class of businessmen with money to spend.
Making money and taking risks was exhilarating and there was an
excitement in the air which, in turn, created a climate which may have
favoured intellectual innovation.   *rise or fall ??*

References

1   D.S. Chambers, *The Imperial Age of Venice 1380-1580* (Thames and
    Hudson, 1970), p. 33.
2   Quoted in Chambers, *Imperial Age*, pp. 38-9.
3   F.C. Lane, *Venice: A Maritime Republic* (John Hopkins University Press,
    1973), pp. 362-4.
4   Luke VI, 35; Deuteronomy XXIII, 19-20.
5   G. Brucker, (ed.) *The Society of Renaissance Florence: a documentary study*
    (Harper and Row, 1971), pp. 93-4.
6   J.A. Schumpeter, *Capitalism, Socialism and Democracy* (Allen and Unwin,
    1943), p. 123.
7   Vespasiano, *Renaissance Princes, Popes, and Prelates* (Harper and Row,
    1963), p. 218.
8   Brucker, *Society of Renaissance Florence*, pp. 15-16.
9   D. Chambers and B. Pullan, (eds), *Venice: A Documentary History 1450-
    1630* (Blackwell, 1992), p. 171.
10 Brucker, *Society of Renaissance Florence*, pp. 23-4.
11 *Ibid.* p. 26.
12 Chambers and Pullan, *Venice*, p. 257.
13 Quoted in Chambers, *Imperial Age*, p. 77.

Summary Diagram
Making Money: The Economic Framework

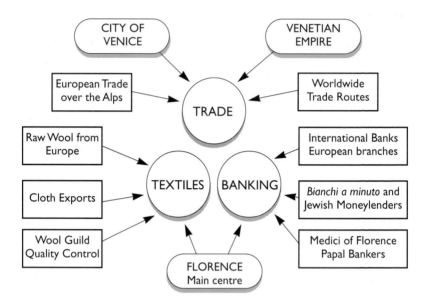

When you have read this chapter, find some of your fellow students who are studying Economics and try to explain to them, in your own words, the main ideas you have learned here. Encourage them to ask you questions about it, and think about how these could be answered.

Answering source-based questions on 'Making Money: The Economic Framework'

1. Money and Religion: The Problem of Usury

Re-read the extract from Vespasiano about Cosimo de' Medici on page 15, then answer the following questions.

a) Why do you think Vespasiano was so hesitant in hinting that Cosimo had been guilty of usury? Try to think of one general reason (legal, religious, social and political) and one reason which was personal to the relationship between Vespasiano and Cosimo. (3 marks)

b) Pope Eugenius was resident in Florence when Cosimo came to power in 1434 and supported him; the Medici were the papal bankers. How do these two facts affect your reading of this extract? (3 marks)

c) What does this passage tell you about the relationship between money and religion in Renaissance Italy? (4 marks)

2. *Attitudes to wealth*

Read the extracts from Dati, Zane, Morelli, della Cueva and Priuli, pages 16-17, then answer the following questions.

a) What do the extracts from Gregorio Dati and Zuare Zane tell us about the risks which businessmen took? Give examples of problems posed by natural disaster, illegal activity and debt. (4 marks)

b) What impression do you get of the character of Giovanni Morelli from his comments? How would you describe his values? (10 marks)

c) What do Don Alonso della Cueva's and Girolamo Priuli's comments tell us about social prestige and money-making? Can you relate this to the idea of the Italian cities having capitalist economies? (6 marks)

To answer successfully any question based on original sources you need to do two things:

1. To place the extract in a wider context which shows what you know about the period in general and the society in which the extract was written. This background material, however, must be relevant to the passage. In question 1 for example, do not try to write down everything you know about Cosimo de' Medici and banking, but explain the law of usury, how it affected Christians and Jews, the economic need for businessmen in a capitalist system to borrow money and so on. In other words, show your awareness of the context of the passage, but ensure that you show clearly why the background points you are making are relevant to the passage in question.

2. You also need to examine the precise wording of the extract and to explain in detail the significance of particular phrases. For example, in question 2 you need to explain the significance of not telling your 'relatives, friends nor partners' how much you are worth, and discuss how crippling a burden taxation really was (or was not). You will not fully understand the importance of some of the points made here, such as 'dowries' and 'the obligations in your father's will' until you have read the next chapter on the Social Fabric. Economic matters cannot be discussed in isolation, but need to be related to social and other issues, so at this early stage any answer must be provisional.

So, to answer properly any question on the sources you need to combine detailed comments on the wording of the extract with background knowledge of the wider context in which it is set. Neither background nor detail is sufficient on its own; aim for a balance between the two, and if you can relate each to the other all the better.

Answering Essay Questions on 'Making Money: The Economic Framework'

The economic issues discussed here need to be related to social, political or cultural ones discussed in later chapters. The questions on Venice and Florence at the end of Chapter four consider the connections with social and political history, and those on patronage at the end of Chapter eight relate economic to cultural issues.

If you want to attempt an essay on this chapter alone, you might ask:
'What were the major differences and similarities between how the rich men of Venice and of Florence made their money?'

But even this question, which is almost entirely an economic one, would be difficult to answer before you have read the next two or three chapters. Although there is not a great deal of *information* you need from the ensuing chapters, there is much *understanding*. It is only when you are aware of the social position and the political power of 'the rich men' referred to in the question that you can discuss their economic practices properly.

There is an important distinction between *knowledge* and *understanding*. To write a decent essay you need both. People who enter quiz competitions need knowledge, so that they can give short factual answers to direct questions. Essay writers need knowledge too (you cannot write a good essay if you do not know any facts), but it is not enough. You also need understanding - a broader and wider awareness of the context into which a piece of knowledge fits. Indeed, there are very few historical facts which are not affected by their context. Things look different and need to be expressed differently depending from where you view them. For example, the facts about usury may be expressed in a slightly different way in essays on Church Law, on the Jews, and on the problems of businessmen in early capitalism. A *fact* would remain the same, of course, but your understanding of the contexts in which that fact was being used would lead you to present it in slightly different ways. By doing that you would show understanding as well as knowledge. If you just learn by rote 'six things you never knew about Cosimo de' Medici' you will still lack understanding; you can acquire that only by reading as much as you can. You could try writing the economic essay suggested above now, and then try it again after you have read the next three chapters and see the difference. That experience should explain to you clearly the point which this paragraph has been trying to make.

3 The Social Fabric

The leading men of a city are sometimes called 'elders' or 'city fathers'. These terms well describe the men who dominated public life in Renaissance Italy. Government and society were patriarchal. Cities were controlled by rich old men, and occasionally by a rich young man. The dominant social institution was the family, a body of immense power and influence ruled by a father or patriarch. Rich old men are defined by gender, age and wealth. Families sought to control women of all ages and younger men, just as society controlled its unruly elements and the poor. Yet women, youths and the poor, although disadvantaged, were not entirely powerless and complex processes of law and social control kept them in order. This chapter examines first the urban family, then looks in turn at each of these potentially disruptive groups: women, young men and the poor.

1 The Urban Family

The Florentine artist Leon Battista Alberti is best known for his theoretical book *On Painting* but he also wrote a long treatise *On the Family*. Like most Florentines, his second allegiance was to his city - his first to his family. The same was true of the people of Venice and the other cities of Renaissance Italy, each of which can be viewed essentially as a loose alliance of great families. No one was more aware than Alberti of the petty squabbles and irritations of family life, but he also knew that the honour of the family and the well-being of its members were the paramount concerns of life. Devotion to the Church and allegiance to the state both mattered greatly, but the family mattered more. 'Never,' he promised, 'as long as there is art or power in me, will I spare myself fatigue or exertion or any strenuous effort that may prove good or useful to the Alberti family.'[1] The support of a family sustained both rich and poor alike. But once again the historian is led to concentrate on the rich because of the availability of surviving evidence. A wealthy man might have many ambitions in life: to be successful in business and make money; to play his part in the government of his city and engage in political life; to support his parents and maintain the honour of his family name; to raise a family and provide for his children. At this time a man's family was more than a domestic backdrop or a private retreat. It was the centre of his life, the thing which defined him, the heart of his identity.

In Venice, sons born into noble families had the right, when adult, to govern the city (see page 39). Therefore their births had to be carefully recorded, by the state as well as the Church. The father, or if he was away from the city the mother or another close relative, was required by law to register the child within eight days of his birth with one of the chief law officers of Venice. The political privilege this involved in Venice made the procedure exceptional, but everywhere birth mattered. Membership of a family bestowed rights and obligations. Men felt it a duty to support their brothers and sisters, physically, mentally and financially.

Marriage was, therefore, a family affair. It was arranged by the family because it affected the whole family. Only when the sense of family is unimportant can marriage concern just the bride and groom. Family honour and prestige, property and credit were involved; marriages forged political alliances and cemented economic partnerships. An inappropriate marriage could damage the status of all the family members and wide consultation and agreement were sought before so important a decision was made. It was unusual for a marriage to be forced on sons or daughters against their will, but they were socialised from birth to accept the partner selected by their family. The twentieth-century notion that falling in love should precede marriage is as much culturally-learned as the Renaissance view that it should follow it.

A marriage entailed a whole set of those rituals and ceremonies which were so important to Renaissance people. There were four main ceremonial stages. First came the *impalmàtura*, when the marriage contract was signed and representatives of the two families - significantly not the bride and groom - would formally shake hands (the Italian word *palmàta* means a slap with the hand). This was the first public stage in the proceedings and often took place in a church or on the steps of a church. But it was a legal, not a religious ceremony, presided over not by a priest but by a lawyer. Secondly came the betrothal when the father of the bride formally presented her to the groom who placed the betrothal ring on her finger. The order of the third and fourth ceremonies varied. There would be a wedding banquet followed by the bride-bed, and there would be a solemn religious service, the Nuptial Mass, which would either precede or follow the party and the consummation. These detailed rituals provided frequent occasions for disputes as etiquette often involved family status and honour. Who should be consulted first? Who should be told when? Where should the betrothal take place? When should the public announcement be made? Should the wedding gown be silk or satin? All were questions fraught with danger. To avoid the risk of the loss of status if a proposal were refused, a marriage broker, a man of high social standing, often the superior of both of the families, would discreetly ensure whether or not such an alliance would be welcome. The status of the marriage partners it could attract was often an indication of whether, socially, a family was on the way up or down. That in turn might affect the credit-worthiness of the family and so its economic viability.

Negotiations centred on the dowry a father would provide with his daughter. Here all the commercial acumen of successful businessmen was employed. It was traditional to provide the couple with a marriage-chest, a *cassone*, in which linen would be stored. These were often elaborate and sometimes decorated by leading artists; Botticelli's painting *Mars and Venus*, now in the National Gallery, London, was originally painted as the front of a wedding-chest. Negotiations would decide whether the cost of the *cassone*, and perhaps of the ring and the gown as well, were to be deducted from the dowry, or to be in addition to it. In the course of the fifteenth century the size of dowries doubled: in Florence whereas 1,000 florins would have been a good dowry in 1400, by 1500 2,000 was becoming common. At the heart of a wedding lay the marriage contract. This was a complex legal document mostly concerned with the dowry, which might well be provided in the form of land and property rather than cash.

Another legal document critical in ordering the affairs of a family was the will of the family head. Often fathers would make elaborate and detailed provisions for their daughters, then, in a single sentence at the end, state that the remainder of their property was to be divided equally between their sons. The disproportionate space should not mislead us: the vast bulk of a family fortune passed in the male line. But the whole estate did not go to the eldest son. Each member of the family would be provided for and no document gives a better picture than wills, of the passionate concern for family of Renaissance fathers.

It used to be assumed that most households were large, extended families. When Iris Origo wrote her fine book on *The Merchant of Prato* in 1957, she stressed that the word *famiglia* was 'used to designate not only a man's immediate descendants, but every relative living under the same roof and eating the same bread - aunts and uncles and cousins and cousins' children, down to the most remote ties of blood.'[2] This was certainly true of Florence and Tuscany in the thirteenth century, and it stayed true of other Italian cities later. In Venice, for example, it remained common for a number of brothers to live together in a single household. But Richard Goldthwaite has argued that in Florence in the fourteenth century 'the individual found his political and legal bonds of loyalty to the family, as those to the guild and other communal corporations, slowly loosened and finally dissolved'.[3] The extended family fragmented and was replaced, he suggested, by small independent households consisting of 'modern' nuclear families. More recent statistical work, based on the Castato tax returns of 1427 in Florence and the Tuscan countryside ruled by the city, has shown that 55 per cent of households consisted of a simple nuclear family - a man and wife with or without children, or children living with one widowed parent. Another 15 per cent of households consisted of a single person, or two unmarried brothers living together. Only 10 per cent of households were the classic 'extended family' consisting of parents, grandparents, uncles, aunts, grandchildren, nephews, nieces, brothers, sisters and cousins.

Statistically, the average size of a household in Tuscany in 1427 was 4.42: 44 per cent of households had fewer than four people in them and 58 per cent had fewer than five. Households of over six people were less than 20 per cent of the total and those of ten or more only 3.6 per cent. Families tended to be larger in the countryside than in the city, and in general the size of the household increased with the wealth of the family. But although they might not have lived in the same house and household, in Florence important families tended to live in the same street, or district of the city. The Medici congregated around the parish church of S. Lorenzo and the Alberti remained in the vicinity of the Franciscan church of S. Croce. The Strozzi family accounted for no fewer than 35 households (in 1378) clustered around the monastery of S. Trinita, near the river Arno.

The concept of a *vendetta*, as a long-standing family blood-feud, is one which is still readily understood. Yet by the Renaissance, it was already in decline. Cases involving leading families in street fighting were falling in number, and the family feud Shakespeare depicts so vividly in *Romeo and Juliet* was more characteristic of the early Renaissance than of the fifteenth century. But although in decline, *vendetta* was by no means extinct. Indeed, weak communes made use of it to regulate mighty families who were out of control, by permitting those they had wronged to pursue a legal *vendetta*. In October 1387, the *Signoria* of Florence barred the members of the Strozzi family from communal office and authorised Giovanni and Piero Lenzi, whom they had been persecuting, to pursue a *vendetta*. The Commune would take no notice of any crimes committed by the Lenzi against the Strozzi. The only way the Strozzi could regain their rights and status in the city was to kill or bring alive to the authorities the two violent members of their family that were causing all the trouble.

Family houses, one of which is illustrated on page 27, served a number of purposes. Street level was often far from salubrious, so the ground floor may well have been used to store the goods in which the family traded, or even be let out to others. The chief public family rooms were likely to be on the first floor with high ceilings and wide windows to let in the light, unless the house was an old one, built when houses needed to be fortresses to keep out the family's enemies. The house might be constructed around a central courtyard to allow light to reach those rooms which did not face the street. On one of the higher floors there may well have been a suite of rooms for the eldest son. At the top of the building might be a penthouse - a colonnaded walk open to the air, sometimes with a sloping roof, where the family could take exercise and enjoy fresh breezes away from the smells at ground level. Thus an anxious father could ensure that his daughter could take the air, without being exposed to the dangers and temptations of the streets.

Palazzo Davanzati, Florence. This family home was built in the 14th century. There was a central courtyard with a well; fireplaces and chimneys were built into the walls. Large windows were filled with glass, a luxury before the 15th century. The ground floor of store-rooms, servants quarters and a stable was, in the 15th century, rented out as three wool shops. The penthouse was a 15th century addition

Orsanmichele, Florence. The businessmen's church. The niches contained statues commissioned by the guilds. The central niche shown here contains Donatello's marble St George commissioned by the Armourers Guild

2 Women

Renaissance Italy was a patriarchal society organised by men for the benefit of men. Women played a subservient role. When a son was born there was widespread rejoicing; the birth of a daughter often gave rise to commiseration. Poor women worked as hard or harder than poor men, often at less prestigious and congenial tasks. Sometimes this reflected their physical strength: women spun thread, men wove cloth. Richer women were excluded from public life and confined within the household. They were usually referred to in terms which defined their relationship to the men who controlled them - daughter, sister, mother or wife. Women who could not be included in any of these categories normally had two options - becoming either a nun or a prostitute. Most women married and married young. The Tuscan Castato of 1427 revealed that the average age of a bride was 18, of a groom 30; 13 per cent of girls married before their 15th birthday, and nearly 90 per cent married at least once between the ages of 15 and 20. By 25 years of age, 97 per cent of women were already married or widowed. A girl unmarried at 30 stood only a one in four chance of finding a husband; for a spinster of 35 the odds were one in ten. Almost all women who did not marry entered convents; there were virtually no permanent spinsters in the community. By comparison more than half of the adult men in Florence were single; men married much later and many remained permanent bachelors.[4]

Dowries were a critical part of a wedding. A father with a large number of daughters found marriage an expensive business. When the money ran out and he could afford no more dowries, then the remaining daughters had to become nuns. Convents became dumping grounds for undowried daughters and the presence of a significant number of nuns with no vocation for the religious life led to a serious fall in the standards of behaviour. In Venice, the patrician diarist Priuli described 15 convents as brothels where well educated girls of good families entertained young men, Venetians and foreigners, for large sums of money. When there were no customers, he claimed, they hired boatmen to satisfy their lusts. Those pious sisters who had a genuine vocation were distressed and a papal nuncio, Alberto Bolognetti, suggested to the Pope that

1   the closest attention should be paid to the inclinations of the girls who are received into convents. Someone should first ascertain whether they are inspired to immure themselves for ever out of pure devotion and the desire to be better placed to serve God, or whether they are
5   being forced to become nuns by the fear of their fathers, who have used threats to make them consent to do so with their tongues, but not with their hearts. For their fathers cannot marry them to their equals because they are not rich enough to do so, and will not marry them to

lesser men for fear of tarnishing the prestige of their families. From this
10 root spring all the disorders in convents.[5]

In Florence, a special fund was established in 1425, the *Monte della
dote*, into which fathers could place a lump sum when a daughter was
born, which would accumulate at compound interest and be withdrawn when the dowry was required. When fathers made their wills,
they often went to considerable lengths to provide for unmarried
daughters. Sums of money were put aside for their dowries, provided,
of course, that they married with the consent of their brothers. The
marriage contract would normally specify that if the wife became a
widow her dowry would be returned to her, to enable her to marry
again. Any sons of the marriage would, of course, remain in their
father's family; their mother could stay with them if she wished but
she would often choose to return to her own family, or even to re-
marry. The will of the Florentine Fetto Ubertini tried to provide for
all eventualities:

I   I bequeath to my wife Pia, daughter of Ubaldo Bertaldi, the sum of 125
    florins in addition to her dowry, and also all of her clothing and acces-
    sories. And if she desires to remain a widow and live with our children,
    she may have an income sufficient to maintain herself and a servant in
5   my house. However, if she withdraws her dowry (from my estate), then
    I cancel the bequest of 125 florins, nor shall she receive living expenses
    for herself and a servant, but only if she leaves her dowry in my estate,
    and remains a widow. To each of my daughters - Filippa, Antonia,
    Francesca, Andrea, and Tommasa - I bequeath the sum of 400 florins for
10 their dowries if they intend to marry, or the sum of 225 florins if they
    become nuns. If my daughters become widows, and wish to return to
    my house, it is my will that they may remain there as long as they wish,
    and if they do not recover their dowry, they shall receive from my estate
    the necessary means to sustain themselves as long as they live.[6]

For a Renaissance woman, marriage meant an almost perpetual
round of pregnancy and childbirth. On 5 November 1445, the
Florentine Luca da Panzano recorded in his diary the death of his
wife. They had been married for just over 20 years and in that time
she had borne him 11 living children. She died in childbed, her
final son stillborn. In addition to the five daughters mentioned in
his will, Fetto Ubertini had eight surviving sons. Such numbers were
not unusual, nor was death in childbirth. Men who lost their wives in
this way grieved, then remarried quickly as someone was needed to
continue to care for the young family. Often wives were the same age
as the oldest of their stepsons. The ability to cope in such circumstances was a quality often sought in a bride. Alessandra Strozzi, on
the look out for a suitable wife for her son, Filippo, reported of one
girl,

> We have information that she is affable and competent. She is respon-
> sible for a large family (there are 12 children, six boys and six girls), and
> the mother is always pregnant and isn't very competent.[7]

Within a family, a wife and mother would exercise a degree of control;
outside of it she was powerless. Life was perhaps worst for young girls
trapped in prostitution. Pimps would seduce and kidnap girls in one
city and remove them to another where they knew no-one outside of
the brothel and had no chance of returning home. The women who
had the greatest degree of control over their lives were wealthy widows
whose husbands had left them property, and the abbesses of convents
whose community was endowed with land. Religious houses, which
might include both reluctant novices and pious, holy women, were
directed sometimes by capable administrators and resourceful
leaders. Few women were more powerful than an intelligent and
ambitious abbess.

3 Young Men

Just as women were excluded from politics and government, so were
young men. In Florence men were prohibited from public life until
the age of 30; in Venice few could take any place in government
before the age of 25 or enjoy real power before they were 50.
Hereditary princes, of course, could inherit when young: Francis I of
France was 20 when he came to the throne; Henry VIII of England
was 17; Charles I of Spain, 15. But when men were elected to office, it
was usually the old who were chosen. Between 1400 and 1600 the
average age of popes at election was 54; that of doges of Venice was 72.
Yet most men were young. The 1427 Castato showed that 44 per cent
of the population of Tuscany were under the age of 20; average life
expectancy was less than 30; men who were 40 and above were
regarded as old. Some lived longer, of course; Michelangelo died at
the age of almost 89, but had described himself as 'old' when he was
42. Aristotle had declared 30 to be the perfect age and this view was
widely accepted by Renaissance men, though most died before they
reached it. Of the 20,000 males in Florence in 1427, 12,000 were
below the age of 30. The problem for the authorities was how these
young men's ambitions were to be contained, their energies
controlled, and their exclusion from public life justified.

As boys grew up they passed through a number of stages, each of
which was named and had suitable public activities attached to it.
Babies might well be called *innocenti*, but children and adolescents
(*fanciulli*) could easily become unruly. From 1410 in Florence a
number of clubs and companies were formed for adolescent boys. At
first they accepted all ages from 13 to 24, but from 1442 onwards
there was separation at the age of 19. The older adolescents from 19
to 24 were described as being 'too old to be among boys, too young to

be among mature men'.[8] In 1427 the average age of men fathering children in Florence was 39 years and 9 months, so most teenage boys had fathers who were either old or, more likely, dead. Unless adolescent males were carefully restrained they could pose a threat to stability in society and order in the state, so these clubs were formed by their elders to act as agents of social control. The fear was that, without this initiative, boys would form their own violent gangs. Indeed that happened in Rome. When Pope Pius II returned to the city in October 1461 after an absence of 33 months, he found it in a state of lawlessness. A gang of 300 boys, from powerful and important families, had graduated from hen-stealing to rape, abduction and murder and were terrorising the city. Pius allowed the gang to carry him in procession across the city on his return, before executing nine ring-leaders and restoring order. In Florence, the clubs channelled adolescent boys' energies into the ritual of church services, of public speaking, of performing plays around the city, and of taking a major part in ceremonial processions.

The term *giovani* described young men from the age of 24 up to about 40, when they became *vecchi* or old. It covered the time both before and after the 'perfect age' of 30 and, in Richard Trexler's words, 'was the period in which the young approached the pinnacle of their physical and mental powers, and receded from it when still potent'.[9] Theoretically, this was the age when men could enter political life, but it was expected that usually real power would still lie with their elders. As Donato Giannotti observed, 'they say the *giovani* should not discuss public affairs, but pursue their sexual needs'.[10] Venice in particular was a gerontocracy - a state ruled by old men. In those parts of government where real power lay, only very few *giovani* were to be found. In the words of a sixteenth-century Venetian,

> the natural coldness of the old comes to be moderated by the heat of the young. Still, these youths are not equal in number to the elderly but just sufficient so that in the Senate's judgements there may be, or appear to be, some sign of heat.[11]

But there was no political or ideological difference between young and old. Neither constituted a faction with a distinct set of policies.

Although it was considered that government required the maturity and wisdom which came with old age, in other ways young men were considered to be technically adult (that is to have reached the age of discretion and legal emancipation) at around the age of 14. At this age, Church law allowed boys to consummate a marriage; girls needed to be only 12. In Florence, young men were taxed and eligible for military service at the age of 18. Boys entered business young. They could become apprentices from the age of seven. Some 13-year-olds were named as the heads of manufacturing companies but this was a legal convenience and we do not know at what age they would have begun to make important decisions. With nearly half the population under the age of 20, young men inevitably grew up quickly. In these circumstances, their exclusion from public life was all the more striking.

4 The Poor

Historians find a depressing similarity in the problems of the poor in whatever society or period they study. People who live close to the margin, who have no reserves for times of illness or unemployment, who depend upon the charity of others and lead generally wretched lives, form the majority in most societies. Renaissance Italy was no exception. Most people were poor. When the harvest failed and life became impossible on the land, rural peasants came into the towns to look for a job. When urban unemployment was bad, the city poor went out into the countryside in search of work and food. Neither really improved their lot.

The needs of the poor are fundamental: work, food, clothing, shelter, companionship. In Florence nearly half of the poor, or the *popolo minuto*, were employed in the manufacture of woollen cloth; 15 per cent worked in menial trades controlled by the other guilds, and another 15 per cent were outside of guild control working as carters, fishermen, grooms, messengers, pedlars, servants and so on. In the district of the city analysed by Brucker, 25 per cent were not identified by occupation in 1379. Some of these moved rapidly from one job to another, others operated as vagrants, vagabonds and beggars, or formed part of the criminal underworld. In Venice, occupations also included shipbuilders, dockers, boatmen and men producing ropes and sails or working in the gunpowder mills or glassworks. In Rome, which lacked both the trade of Venice and the manufactures of Florence, there was a greater dependence on the provision of services. The poor worked as stablemen and servants, shopkeepers, tanners of leather and millers, whose water mills were clustered together on an island in the river Tiber. A large number were employed in meeting the various needs of the hordes of pilgrims who visited the city from all over Europe. In the years after the Sack of Rome in 1527, many were employed as labourers in the rebuilding of the city.

The attitudes of the rich to the poor were dominated by the duty of Christian charity and the fear of disorder. Both led them to feed the poor in times of famine, and to this end secret grain supplies were hidden in the cities. Two comments, one from Venice and the other from Florence, illustrate this dual motivation. In Florence in June 1417 with plague imminent, a member of the city government pointed out the necessity 'to provide for the preservation of our regime' and argued,

First, we should acknowledge our obligation to God, taking into account the poverty of many, that is, by distributing alms to the needy. But since not all are quiet, and in order to instill fear into some, foot-soldiers should be hired who will serve the needs of the Commune.[12]

In Venice, in October 1569, a banker in the city recorded

1   the worst shortage of bread and flour ever seen within the memories even of aged men. For six days on end there was no bread in the bakers' shops and no flour in the warehouses, so that the poor could not buy victuals in any part of the city. If the hardship had lasted even a little
5   longer, disturbances would have been seen throughout Venice. [The government] sent state flour to the warehouses every day, and there was a great tumult on account of the great crowd of people who wanted to buy flour. [They] had to station men at the doors of the warehouses to act as guard, for the city was already beginning to riot.[13]

The poor's potential for riot was ever-present, but throughout the Renaissance it was kept well under control by the authorities. In Florence, the lower orders staged one major revolt in 1378. The poorer employees of the guild members, chiefly the Wool Guild, and those craftsmen with no guild, sought to have some say in the government of the city. They elected as their leader Michele di Lando, a wool comber and son of a woman who sold provisions to the prisoners in the state jail. First they took over the *Bargello*, the palace fortress where the law officers of the city resided. They then invaded the palace of the *signoria*, from which the city was governed. Michele was proclaimed Lord of Florence, but his lordship lasted only two more days. After this Revolt of the Ciompi had been put down, fairly easily, by the Florentine Commune, the city was never seriously threatened by an uprising of the poor. In Venice, things were not allowed to get even that far. Brutal public executions to discourage potential rioters were common. In more peaceful times, the duty of Christian charity was not neglected by individuals or institutions. Men joined together in social clubs, usually based on their parish church and known as confraternities, which engaged in charitable work. But they took care, as the rich have in all ages, to distinguish between the deserving and undeserving poor, between Christ's poor and the devil's poor, between the genuinely needy and those they regarded as scroungers.

5 Conclusion

For so dynamic an age, Renaissance society was surprisingly stable. For both rich and poor - but particularly for the rich - the family was the dominant social grouping. Membership of the local parish church, of a guild, of a confraternity, even of a state, was far less significant to individuals than their membership of a family. Pride in the family's past, and support for its present members were pre-eminent in the concerns of the people of Renaissance Italy. In Florence and Tuscany, the extended family living in the same household was largely replaced by nuclear families, possibly giving more scope for the development of the individual, but the larger family or clan remained a crucially important unit even when it was divided into a number of smaller households. There were, of course, tensions between different classes, genders and ages, but for almost everyone the family was the focal point of unity. Generally speaking, the poor were kept well under control; famine and want rather than discontent and ambition were perceived to be the things most likely to lead to unrest. Socialisation more than law was relied on to keep women in their place, which was seen as firmly in the private sphere of life. Within that limitation, fathers usually showed real concern for their daughters' well-being, though economic pressures and the need for expensive dowries might lead to some of them being forced to become reluctant nuns for the good of the family. In the republics of Florence and Venice, the main threat to stability was posed by rich young men excluded from government, but an elaborate system of youth organisations provided a network of agencies of social control to keep them in order. So, Italian Renaissance society was dominated by rich old men - the heads of leading families. How far their economic power and social ascendancy was also reflected in political mastery is the theme of the next chapter.

References

1   L.B. Alberti, *The Family in Renaissance Florence* (University of South Carolina Press, 1969), p. 32. This is a translation of *On the Family.*
2   I. Origo, *The Merchant of Prato: Francesco di Marco Datini* (Cape, 1957; reprinted Penguin Books, 1963), p. 181.
3   R. Goldthwaite, *Private Wealth in Renaissance Florence: a study of four families* (Princeton University Press, 1968), p. 252.
4   D. Herlihy and C. Klapisch-Zuber, *Tuscans and their Families: A Study of the Florentine Castato of 1427* (Yale University Press, 1985), pp. 202-15.
5   Chambers and Pullan, *Venice,* p. 208.
6   Brucker, *Society of Renaissance Florence,* pp. 50-1.
7   *Ibid.* pp. 38-9.
8   Richard Trexler, *Public Life in Renaissance Florence* (Cornell University Press, 1980), p. 371.
9   *Ibid,* p. 388.
10 *Ibid,* p. 387.
11 R. Finlay, *Politics in Renaissance Venice* (Benn, 1980), p. 127.
12 Brucker, *Society of Renaissance Florence,* p. 230.
13 Chambers and Pullan, *Venice,* pp. 108-9.

Summary Diagram
The Social Fabric

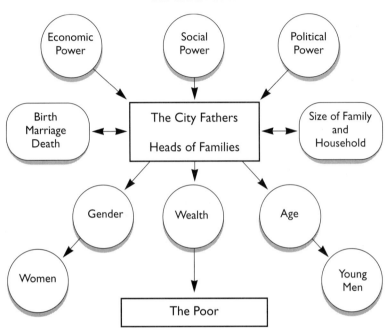

When you have read this chapter, find some of your fellow students who are studying Sociology and try to explain to them, in your own words, the main ideas you have learned here. Encourage them to ask you questions about it, and think how these could be answered.

Answering source-based questions on 'The Social Fabric'

1. The role of women in the family and in society
Read the extracts from Bolognetti, Ubertini and Strozzi, pages 28-30, then answer the following questions.
a) How far do you think Alberto Bolognetti's anxiety was motivated by concern for the girls, their families or the Church? (5 marks)
b) What attitudes to his wife and daughters are revealed in Fetto Ubertini's will? (10 marks)
c) How far do Alessandra Strozzi's comments reflect the criteria used in selecting a bride? Discuss what other factors were important. (5 marks)

2. Attitudes to the poor
Read the extracts on pages 32-3, then answer the following questions.
a) What evidence is there that the poor were considered a threat to the stability of society and of the state? (4 marks)

b) Discuss the relative importance of Christian duty, compassion, and fear in persuading the rich to help the poor. (6 marks)

Answering essay questions on 'The Social Fabric'

1. Why was marriage such a complex business for rich families in Renaissance Italy?
2. Examine the importance of the family as a social, economic and political unit in Renaissance Florence. (To answer the last part of this question, you will need to read Chapter four).

An essay is a very different thing from a chapter in a book. A chapter seeks to be broad, general, open-ended and a part of a larger whole; an essay is self-contained, specific, closely related to a question. A chapter presents information which the reader can use in a variety of ways; an essay gives readers far fewer options and directs their thinking along a clear route. Books inform readers about a topic; essays argue a case.

We all know that you do not get questions like 'write down everything you know about marriage in Renaissance Italy' and we laugh at the idea, but when some students see question 1 they will focus on the single word 'marriage' in it and proceed to write down everything they know about marriage in Renaissance Italy. Although they may present the reader with a lot of accurate facts, many of which might be relevant to an essay on this topic, it will not be a good essay unless they *use* the facts to answer the question. Some bad essays are rather like a 'do-it-yourself kit': all the facts are there which are needed to answer the question, but it is left to the reader to do the work. The art of essay writing is to *use* the information in a specific way to answer a precise question. It is no good copying bits out of books - this is called plagiarism and it is stealing someone else's intellectual property. But it is not only an improper thing to do, it is also useless. You need to *use* the information that is presented in a general way in books to answer a specific question. To copy bits out and string them together doesn't do the job of answering the question. So, how do you write an essay?

First, read as many books as possible and make notes *in your own words*. It is essential that you put the information into your own words at this stage; it is hard work but it pays off in the long run. Try to read a general book (like this one) first and make detailed notes on it; then as you read more specialised books you can make fewer notes and can concentrate on points you think will be relevant to your essay.

When you have finished your reading, sit down and read through all your notes twice. Think of the main themes and big issues that you have enough information to write a paragraph on if you needed to, like 'the dowry', 'the importance of ceremony and ritual', 'the concern and involvement of all the family members' and so on.

Look carefully at the question - at the words in it and at the sentence structure. A question which asks 'how...?' requires a very different answer from one which asks 'why...?'; look carefully at any adjectives or adverbs which qualify important nouns and verbs. In question 1 the adjective 'complex' is important, but do not forget to discuss the implications of the noun 'business' as well. Often the question will dictate the structure of the answer; in question 2 you clearly need to have major sections on economic, social and political issues - and don't forget to discuss what a 'unit' means.

When the precise question is firmly fixed in your mind, you need to think about how best to use the information in your notes to answer it. Some people find it helpful to think this out away from their notes, so take a walk (or a bath) - on your own - and try to work out in your head the structure of an essay which will answer the question. When you get home (or dry) write this plan down, plus, if you can, one or two alternatives to it. Leave it for a day or two and work on something else. Then make a final decision on the structure of your essay.

The plan you draw up for your essay should consist of subheadings for each paragraph (you will not put the subheadings into the finished piece of work, of course, but you need to know what they are). Do not have too many paragraphs. It will depend on the essay, but usually between six and ten (plus an introduction and conclusion) will be right.

When you have decided on the paragraph headings, read through your notes again and mark in the margin (with a separate code for each paragraph) everywhere there is some relevant information you can use.

When you come to write a paragraph, using your marginal key, read all the bits (from a number of different books) which are relevant to this paragraph. Look at the question again. Then write a paragraph in your own words using information from the books to answer the question. The first sentence of the paragraph should set out clearly what you will do in that paragraph. The final sentence of the paragraph should show how that paragraph has been relevant to the question. If you find you cannot relate the paragraph to the question, then leave it out. Do not put it in just because you have done the work on it and do not want to waste it - after all, if you were making a fruitcake you would not put a tin of sardines in it just because you had one around, would you?

Mark Twain once apologised to his mother for writing her a long letter, saying that he didn't have time to write a short one. A long essay, which just throws everything in, is easier to write than a short one which selects and orders its material carefully, but it is not as effective in answering the question. Your essay should be a surgeon's scalpel, not a thug's blunt instrument. You should spend more time planning your essay than writing it. If you plan it properly, it will write itself.

4 The Political Structure

The economic and social power structures, which were examined in the last two chapters, influenced how the Italian states were governed because political forms reflected the interests of the rich and powerful. Just as economic practices were innovative and society dynamic, so politics and government were characterised by variety and change. Within the Italian peninsula we find the most stable republic in the world (Venice) and one of the most backward feudal monarchies (Naples), weak faction-ridden city states (like Genoa) and a modern princedom at the cutting-edge of bureaucratic and administrative reform (Milan). Somewhere between them was the government of Florence, where the conflict between the old and new politics was not properly resolved until the end of the period. Generally speaking, there is a trend from republican government, in which all the leading citizens played a part, to the princely rule of a single family. But this movement was not universal and we must be careful not to make everything fit this pattern. To be able to discuss these developments properly, we need first to look at the form of government in each of the major states.

1 The Republic of Venice

The city of Venice sat between maritime empire and *terraferma*, between land and sea, impregnable to attack by either army or navy. Perched in a lagoon into which three rivers flowed, protected by islands and the Lido from the tides of the Adriatic, no bridge then connected it with the mainland. Often threatened, Venice was never captured in the thousand years from its foundation to 1797, when Napoleon's troops entered the city. Venice was a byword for stability and order.

a) Politics and Society

Renaissance Venice was a republic but not a democracy. It had no king or prince, but neither was power in the hands of most of the people. Venice was ruled by its most eminent families. From the foundation of the city until the 1290s, whoever happened to be the most powerful and wealthy citizens ruled the state. Then the names of the dominant families were set down (a generation later they were written in the first Golden Book) and participation in government was limited to the adult males of those houses. This process was known as the *serràta* (the word in Italian means a closure or a lock-out); thereafter the constitution was closed and confined to those leading families. The *serràta* established the membership of the Patriciate. The Venetian Patricians (those who claimed descent from the original founders of the city) had no titles of nobility; they were citizens of the republic. But their power and dignity were greater than that of the nobility of most other states. Drawn from around 150 families, they controlled the city politically and dominated it socially. Patrician culture ruled supreme. Economically, they were intimately involved in the commercial life of the Empire. Of course, not all patricians were equal. Some were wealthy and others impoverished; some families (one historian suggests about 40[1]) traditionally dominated the government. Because all of the sons of the 150 or so named families, not just the eldest, became patricians, the number of individuals increased dramatically to over 2,600 in 1513.

In most states, political power rests with the socially prominent and the economically powerful. As wealth and status change so does the political control which accompanies them. When a system of government is closed, however, as Venice was by the *serràta*, there is a serious danger that the upwardly-mobile newly-rich become discontented at their exclusion and create instability. Whilst Venice added very few names indeed to the families of the Patriciate, she largely avoided this danger by the creation of a second rank of privilege. The Citizenry was open to wealthy newcomers and made up about ten per cent of the population. It was from the ranks of the Citizenry that the Venetian civil service was drawn and most of its members were satisfied with the opportunity to become powerful bureaucrats.

b) The Structure of Government

The Venetian constitution has often - too often - been described as a pyramid with the Doge of Venice at its head and the Great Council as its base. This analogy does not work particularly well for the bits in between, but the Great Council was certainly the foundation on which all else was built. Every adult male patrician was a member of the Great Council. This was, of course, only two per cent of the population of the city, let alone the Empire, but Venetian government was still more broadly based than that of any other major Italian state. By the middle of the fifteenth century the Great Council had a membership of over 2,000. They met, usually every Sunday afternoon, in a huge hall in the Doge's Palace, to hold elections. They elected the Doge; they elected 60 members of the Senate; they elected the Council of Ten; they even elected the captains of the galley fleets. Indeed, over 800 jobs had to be filled. Some patricians moaned that they did nothing but vote. Because the Great Council was too large to be an effective legislature, it was the Senate which became the central decision-making body in the constitution - 'the council which governs our state'.[2] Every year, in August and September, the Great Council would elect 60 senators who would choose another 60 to join them, and to these would be added around 100 more office holders who had a right to sit in the Senate. The senators had a profound sense of dignity and a reputation for wisdom which stretched as far as England (Shakespeare makes Othello refer to the Venetian senators as 'most potent, grave and reverend signiors'[3]). Senators sat in carved seats around the walls of their chamber and here major issues were discussed and great policies decided.

The head of state was the Doge of Venice. He was elected for life, but could be disposed of if he proved unsatisfactory. Doges were elected by a complex procedure which combined the chance of a lottery with the judgement of the patricians. How powerful the Doge was depended very much on the man elected. If a weak man was chosen, he would be no more than a figurehead, whereas a powerful and ambitious man, like Francesco Foscari, could make the Doge a leader to be reckoned with. However a doge had to act within strict constitutional limits, and if he over-stepped these he could be deposed - as Foscari was in 1457. Such events were rare. Most doges knew their place. The real executive was not the Doge but the *Collegio*, which has been called 'the steering committee of the Senate'.[4] This was a council of 26, made up of the Doge and the three chief judges of the criminal court together with representatives of the six parts of the city, and of a range of patrician families. Five members of the *Collegio* were less experienced men who dealt only with the maritime empire. The *Collegio* was a part of both the Senate and of the Great Council and sat in state in each of these assemblies on a dais at the end of the hall. They conducted the day-to-day business affairs. Every morning they would go to the Doge's Palace, and sit with him to receive petitions from the public. Then, in private, they would consider the letters received since yesterday and decide which should be presented to the Senate. This would lead to a more general discussion of matters of state in a relatively informal setting:

> it should be known that when the Doge speaks to Senate or to the Great Council he stands up and faces straight ahead, never moving from his place, but in the Council of Ten and the Collegio he speaks sitting down.'[5]

The Council of Ten was by far the most important of a large number of small committees dealing with particular issues. It was elected by the Great Council, but its members had to be senators. It was concerned mainly with state security, stability and the defence of the established constitution. It had a sinister reputation. Rumours abounded of men suspected of subversion being brought before it by night and quietly disposed of in the lagoon. Marin Sanudo, one of the leading patricians in the early-sixteenth century, described it as 'a very severe magistracy' and went on:

> i those who fall in the hands of the Council of Ten cannot defend themselves with lawyers; when they examine a case they block [access to] the Palace, and there are four persons delegated who act for the

5 defence, if they are so willing; and whatever is decided by the Council of Ten is firm and valid and cannot be revoked... This Council imposes banishment and exile upon nobles, and has others burned and hanged if they deserve it, and has authority to dismiss the Prince [Doge], even to do other things to him if he so deserves. Long ago in 1355 a Doge's head was cut off by order of this Council, and in 1457 another was dismissed

10 for being incapable of exercising his duties as Doge... It is laid down that the Council of Ten meets every Wednesday, so that, meeting so often, there should not be a great terror in the city whenever it is called... It is, in conclusion, a very terrifying magistracy, and the Council is highly secret.[6]

In his important study of *Violence in Early Renaissance Venice*, Guido Ruggiero shows that the chief rigours of the law were reserved for those who were seen to threaten the safety and stability of the state. When that happened, the individual, be he rich or poor (he was usually male), was shown little mercy. The violence of the crime was frequently outdone by the violence of the punishment. Ruggiero argues that, in common with Florence and other cities of northern Italy, Venice saw that 'the merchant-banker élite required a more controlled environment'.[7] The city government was becoming more powerful and the independence of the leading families was being curbed.

c) The Myth of Venice

Aristotle (384-322 BC) said that there were three possible forms of government - monarchy, aristocracy and democracy - each of which could be good or bad. Venetians believed their constitution combined the best of each in Doge, Senate and Great Council. Other Italian states (notoriously faction-ridden) openly admired the stability, peace and justice which the Venetian constitution appeared to give the city. Indeed, Venice was widely regarded as having the finest constitution in the world. This 'Myth of Venice' was encouraged by the city, but the reality was less edifying. Votes in the Great Council were bought and sold. Gossip, lobbying and deals abounded, inefficiency was common and generally power lay in the hands of a minority of rich patricians. Stability rested as much on the repressive activity of the Council of Ten as on the perfect constitution. The term 'Myth of Venice' is a creation of modern historians[8], but many contemporaries recognised that the reality did not match the reputation, and the Venetian state consciously set out to propagate the 'myth'. But we must be careful not to take a proper cynicism to excess. The myth mattered. Although contemporaries knew well that the reality was more sordid, it represented the values and the aspirations of Venetians, and of most Italians as well. Certainly, Venice came closer to realising the mythical virtues than most other Italian states.

2 The Greater Princedoms: Naples and Milan

Venice was unique. It was really the only true republic in Italy or perhaps the world. Elsewhere, just as the father was regarded as the natural head of a family, so was a prince seen as the natural head of a state. There were many lesser princedoms in Renaissance Italy, and two great ones - Naples and Milan.

a) The Kingdom of Naples

If Italy is seen as a leg, everything from the knee downwards was the Kingdom of Naples. The king's court and the city of Naples were major centres of artistic, scholarly and cultural life. But outside that single city, the Kingdom played no part in the 'Renaissance'. Politically, as well as culturally and economically, it was backward. A remote, anarchic state, it was more like the feudal monarchies of medieval England and France than the modern city states of Renaissance Italy. Communications were extremely poor in this vast sprawling land and the barons were very much a law unto themselves in their own territory. Naples was a difficult kingdom to rule.

Queen Giovanna II (1414-35) enjoyed passionate affairs with a number of men. As she indulged herself, the Neapolitan barons reduced the Kingdom to a state of anarchy. To bolster her position, Giovanna made a deal with Alfonso of Aragon. He would bring an army to Naples and re-establish royal power; in return, the childless Giovanna would name him as her heir. Alfonso fulfilled his part of the arrangement effectively - although the Queen had not reckoned on his imprisoning her current lover. But when she died, Giovanna left a will leaving the Kingdom to the young brother-in-law of the King of France, René of Anjou. Apart from the will, there was an impossibly complicated tangle of dynastic claims (Giovanna's father had earlier defeated René's grandfather in a struggle for the throne). This chaos was resolved with René's defeat in a seven year war of succession (1435-42) and Alfonso was crowned King of Naples. Alfonso and his illegitimate son Ferrante, who succeeded him, ruled Naples for over 50 years. Both were strong and capable monarchs who kept the barons more or less under control. They made some attempt to reform the government, but failed to make Naples a modern centralised state. Alfonso established a spectacular Renaissance Court in the city of Naples, but most of the Kingdom remained feudal and undeveloped. The French claim to Naples was revived in 1494 (see page 88) and a period of instability ensued from which Ferdinand of Aragon, a cousin of Alfonso, emerged as King of Naples in 1504. He was a shrewd and ruthless ruler whom Machiavelli said 'never preaches anything except peace and good faith; and he is an enemy of both one and the other'.[9]

b) The Duchy of Milan

The confusion that was Naples was quite untypical of Renaissance Italy; much more characteristic were developments in Milan, where three outstanding dukes modernised and centralised government.

```
              The Rulers of Milan 1385-1500

  1     The Visconti Family 1311-1447
        1385-1402   Giangaleazzo Visconti; 1395 First duke of Milan
        1402-1412   Giovanni Maria Visconti
        1412-1447   Filippo Maria Visconti

  2     The Ambrosian Republic 1447-1450

  3     The Sforza Family 1450-1500
        1450-1466   Francesco Sforza
        1466-1476   Galeazzo Maria Sforza - assassinated
        1476-1494   Giovan Galeazzo Sforza
        1494-1500   Lodovico Il Moro Sforza - deposed by the French
```

The old feudal family of the Visconti created, from a collection of separate cities, a single state with an efficient central government. In 1385 Giangaleazzo Visconti murdered his uncle and united the Visconti lands which had previously been ruled by different members of his family. Soon he was master of the whole North Italian Plain, from the Alps to the Apennines and the Adriatic. In 1395 he was 'given' the title of Duke by the Holy Roman Emperor after a large sum of money had changed hands. Venice was impregnable in her lagoon, so next Duke Giangaleazzo, seeking to expand his territory still further, looked south. In 1402 he crossed the Apennines and was soon camped in the hills around Florence. The city lay helpless and could have been taken the next day if the Duke had not died overnight and his expedition collapsed. A generation later, Duke Filippo Maria re-established Visconti power but posed no real threat to Florence. His main achievement was the establishment of a modern administrative framework of government with a centralised bureaucracy. The old feudal privileges of powerful families and the local rights of small cities over taxation, law and order and so on, gave way to a privy council, chancellery and exchequer in Milan which concentrated real power in the hands of the duke. On paper at least, there was an orderly and close-knit governmental structure with clear lines of responsibility and control. Even if this did not always work so well in practice, it was still one of the first modern bureaucracies in Europe. The contrast with Naples could not have been greater.

Filippo died leaving no legitimate male heir and with him the line of the Visconti failed. The following day the Ambrosian Republic was proclaimed. It was dreamed-up by a group of unrealistic scholars and named after the legendary food of the classical gods - ambrosia. But there was no republican tradition to sustain it, no common purpose to unite it. Romantic nostalgia was no substitute for hard political power. Needing an army to defend themselves against the Venetians, they employed a leading mercenary captain (see page 90), Francesco Sforza, to fight for them. In just over two years, the Republic's Assembly of the People had to accept Sforza as Duke of Milan.

Duke Francesco Sforza was a great soldier and a powerful ruler. He retained a large standing army, and the Sforza castle he built in the heart of Milan is one of the major achievements of military architecture in Renaissance Italy. He was also an astute politician. He maintained and developed the centralised institutions of Filippo Visconti. In a master-stroke of diplomacy, he persuaded Cosimo de' Medici to switch Florentine support from Venice to Milan. From the Pope he won the right to appoint all major churchmen in his lands; his brother became Archbishop of Milan. Duke Francesco and his son, who succeeded him, were also patrons of artists and scholars and amongst the greatest of Renaissance builders. The assassination of his son in 1476 brought to the Dukedom Francesco's seven-year-old grandson, Giovan Galeazzo. He was a sickly youth, and real power lay in the hands of his uncle, Lodovico, known because of his dark complexion as 'the Moor' (*Il Moro*). A contemporary of Richard III of England, Lodovico had a sinister reputation which was undeserved; he was a major patron of artists and scholars. But when his nephew died and he succeeded to the dukedom in 1494 many were suspicious. The finest sixteenth-century historian, a Florentine, reported,

> A rumour was spread that the death of Giovan Galeazzo had been caused by immoderate copulation, but it was believed throughout Italy that he had died not from natural causes or sexual excess, but from poisoning.[10]

Lodovico was to acquire even more notoriety as the duke of Milan who invited the French to invade Italy in 1494. He had hoped to get some support in his dealing with the other Italian princes but brought down a hornet's nest on his own head. Although the consequences of that invasion were immense, recent historians have pointed out this notoriety too was undeserved (see page 88). Lodovico was one in a long line of Italian princes who invited in foreigners; he was just unfortunate in having his invitation accepted.

3 The Lesser Princedoms: The Rise of the *Signori*

In medieval Italy there were a large number of independent city-state republics. Government was by the *commune*, through councils of the people, which took a range of forms but always represented the wealthy leading citizens; in no modern sense were they 'democratic'. In the fourteenth and fifteenth centuries, one family in each city state emerged as the dominant political force. Councils were often retained but became no more than rubber stamps, the facade behind which despotic power was established. In a large proportion of states the head of the dominant family became recognised as the lord (the Italian word is *signore*) and in some the family would purchase a title of nobility from the Holy Roman Emperor and become counts, marquises or dukes. This movement from communal republics to hereditary despots has been called 'the rise of the *signori*'.

This took place in the north Italian plain, in Tuscany and in the Papal States; everywhere north of the kingdom of Naples. In the Papal States the *signori* recognised the pope as their formal overlord but in fact enjoyed almost complete independence. Occasionally a pope, like Alexander VI or Julius II, would mount a military expedition to try to re-establish papal authority but the effects were generally short lived (see pages 59-61). In Urbino, Federigo da Montefeltro (see the illustration on page 85), first as *Signore* then as Duke, ruled supreme and established one of the major Renaissance courts, a centre of art and learning. In Bologna the picture was more complex. In the fourteenth century the city freed itself from direct papal rule and a free commune was established. But soon this was dominated first by 16 families, then by one - the Bentivoglio of Bologna who never became formal *signori* but ruled the city for over 60 years, before Julius II re-established direct papal control. In the North Italian Plain, cities struggled to retain their independence from the might of Milan in the west and Venice in the east. Mantua had the strategic advantage of being almost entirely surrounded by water, nestling between a river and a lake. Here the Gonzaga family took control in the early fourteenth century and built a huge, rambling Renaissance palace which still dominates the heart of the town. Some members of the family were brutal soldiers, others cultured patrons of the arts, and between them they built a glittering Renaissance court within a military fortress. At Ferrara, 45 miles down the valley, the Este family had dominated the city since the middle of the thirteenth century, and in 1332 became the first of the Italian *signori* to purchase the title of marquis. This rise of the *signori* provides the context in which we must view the politics of Florence.

4 The Florentine Republic and the Medici

Florence remained a republic. Although the Medici family dominated its government from 1434 to 1494 they always had to show proper respect for the city's republican traditions. In a sense, the Medici were like the *signori* who came first to dominate, and then to rule over, other city states. But there were many great families in Florence, proud of their place as part of the political nation, and the Medici had to tread carefully. Like Venice, Florence was a republic, but her republican institutions were less stable, less confident. Florentines were obsessed with the fear that one faction, one family, would take control - and the formal structure of government showed it.

a) The Constitution

It was, in part, the weakness of the constitution that allowed the Medici family to manipulate it so successfully. Membership of the political nation was fluid and reflected, much better than in Venice, changing economic fortunes. Political power mirrored economic power directly because the right to participate in government lay in membership of the guilds (see page 13). The city was ruled by a nine-man *signoria* made up of the *Gonfalonier* (standard-bearer) of Justice, who was the head of state, six men chosen from the seven leading guilds and two men from the 14 minor guilds. There were various committees which dealt with specific issues such as war (the Ten) or security (the Eight). There were also two legislative councils which had to approve new laws but otherwise had limited power. Both of these were elected by the *signoria*. The fear of faction showed itself in two ways, both of which made Florentine Government unstable. First, the members of the *signoria* were to be chosen entirely by lottery. As John Hale puts it, 'the fortunes of the city which housed some of the wealthiest businesses and the most vivid culture in Europe depended, month by month, on a form of roulette.'[11] Bags were filled with tickets bearing the names of guild members, one bag for the head of state, one for the major guilds and so on. Names were drawn from the bags and, provided the men concerned were not in debt to the state, or dead, they served on the *signoria*. Secondly, this happened every two months. The entire personnel of government, including the head of state, changed six times each year. No-one was eligible for re-election for three years. Designed to prevent a faction entrenching itself, this system made Florentine government dangerously unstable.

Or it would have done, if it had not been subverted. Critical to the whole process were the names in the bags. When it was necessary to update them the bags would be emptied, the names of the dead removed, and new names added. This process was called a scrutiny. A full scrutiny might take many months (the Medici could make it last years) and during this time the officials carrying out the scrutiny would choose the *signoria* with all the names open before them. This was known as election *a mano*, or by hand. The right to hold a scrutiny was conferred by an extraordinary meeting called a *parlemento*. The bells on the tower of the palace of the *signoria* would ring out over the city. The people of Florence would flood into the *Piazza della Signoria* (see the illustration on page 63). The leaders of the regime would come out onto the balcony of the palace and ask the people to approve the setting up of a state of emergency so that a scrutiny could be held. The people, often urged on by troops, would cry their assent, and thus the process was legitimised. Others used this method before the Medici, but they perfected it to an art form.

Florence was obsessed with the fear of faction. The same thinking which decreed that the *signoria* should be chosen by lot every two months, laid down that the three law officers responsible for keeping order should be foreigners appointed for only six months. It was assumed that any Florentine would favour his own family, and that after six months a foreigner would have established local ties which could compromise his impartiality. The powers given to the law officers were considered too extensive to take such a risk. They were established in the palace fortress of the *Bargello*, just a few streets away from the palace of the *signoria*; each of them had a retinue of armed men at their disposal. They investigated complaints as well as hearing cases and pronouncing judgement. The three Florentine law officers were the podestà (the most important law officer), the captain of the popolo (who dealt with the poor), and the executor of the ordinances of justice (who tried to keep the leading families in order).

b) The Medici

The Medici were not one of the oldest Florentine families, but they became the richest. They originated from the countryside 20 miles north-east of Florence and arrived in the city in the early thirteenth century. Within 200 years they had established themselves as international bankers of the first rank and Cosimo de' Medici's father became banker to the papacy. Such a powerful family inevitably made enemies and in 1433 Cosimo was exiled from the city, only to return in triumph the following year. For the next 60 years the Medici dominated Florentine government and the head of the family was seen by foreigners as the ruler of Florence.

Contemporaries' views of Cosimo depended very much on who they were. Pope Pius II was a foreigner, born in Siena, just south of Florence. He was 16 years younger than Cosimo, though they died in the same year. To him, Cosimo was clearly the ruler of the city:

> He was regarded as the arbiter of war and peace, the regulator of law; not so much a citizen as the master of his city. Political councils were held at his house; the magistrates he nominated were elected; he was king in all but name and state.[12]

Niccolò Machiavelli was born five years after Cosimo's death and grew up in the Florence dominated by his grandson Lorenzo. At heart he disliked Medici government, but personal ambition made him curb this emotion. His *History of Florence* was written for a Medici patron and he hoped for more employment from the family, so in his description of Cosimo he chose his words carefully:

1 ... not only was he superior to his contemporaries in influence and
  riches, but also in wisdom and generosity, and it was this generosity
  which distinguished him among the princes of his time... there was
  scarcely a citizen of any position in Florence on whom Cosimo had not
5 bestowed large sums of money... although he was the chief man in
  Florence, he never overstepped the bounds of prudence. In his way of
  living, in servants, equipages, and in all other lines of conduct, he never
  appeared anything but a simple citizen.[13]

Vespasiano da Bisticci, a born flatterer, was a bookseller in Florence
and the Medici were among his best customers. He knew Cosimo well
and was writing in the days of Lorenzo. He recalled the gossip of how
Cosimo had spoken to one of the 'chief citizens' of Florence who had
criticised him and he put these words into Cosimo's mouth:

1 ... it seems to me only just and honest that I should prefer the good
  name and honour of my house to you: that I should work for my own
  interest rather than for yours. So you and I will act like two big dogs
  who, when they meet, smell one another and then, because they both
5 have teeth, go their ways. Wherefore now you can attend to your affairs
  and I to mine.[14]

But Cosimo summed up his own position best when Francesco Sforza
begged a political favour. He pointed out to the Duke of Milan that 'a
republic cannot be run in the same way as a despotic regime'.[15]

Cosimo de' Medici ran Florence from behind the scenes. In the 30
years during which he was the leading citizen of the republic (1434-
64), he took office as head of state only three times - for a total of six
months. He was a man who preferred the quiet reality of power to its
ostentatious display. Members of one *signoria* after another would
seek his advice, either in a semi-formal *ad hoc* body called to debate
and advise, or in the streets as he walked home from church, or
privately in the Medici palace. Time and again, Medici supporters
filled the important positions of the state and Cosimo's wisdom and
judgement guided Florence. The Medici were merchants, bankers
and manufacturers and so could be relied upon to do what was in the
interest of those other merchants, bankers and manufacturers who
were the republic's leading citizens.

Cosimo's grandson Lorenzo, on the other hand, was born to power.
Where Cosimo ruled from the background, Lorenzo gloried in the
full light of publicity. Instead of the usual marriage into a rich
Florentine merchant family, he made a dynastic match with Clarice
Orsini, daughter of one of the major Roman barons. He conducted
foreign policy as if he was the prince of Florence, negotiating directly
with other powers then getting the *signoria* to rubber-stamp his
actions. He was an intellectual and a poet. He wrote both thoughtful
neoplatonic love poetry and bawdy ditties to be sung during the
excesses of Carnival - an indulgence he encouraged. He was a patron

of scholars and artists and it is easy to understand why nineteenth-century historians spoke of the golden age of Lorenzo the Magnificent. But his household was smaller than a princely court and *Magnifico* was a common term of respect used to describe leading men of the age. Lorenzo was part of that world, but neither established nor presided over it. The quarter of a century when he ruled Florence - 1469-92 - was not much more 'golden' than the ones before and after.

However glittering he appeared to foreigners, in the city the opposition to Medici power was plain to see. The Medici needed to control every *signoria* elected - six times a year for 60 years - so the process of manipulation demanded constant attention. In 1458 Cosimo established a new body, the Council of 100, designed to act as a Medici power base. But the family's grip on it kept loosening and Lorenzo had first to reform it in 1471 and then effectively to replace it in 1480 with the Council of 70. More dramatic was the Pazzi conspiracy of 1478. The Pazzi, one of the oldest of Florentine families, and others planned to assassinate Lorenzo and his brother Giuliano in Florence Cathedral. As high mass drew to a close, the assassins struck. Giuliano was killed, but a wounded Lorenzo escaped to rally support and eventually execute over 70 conspirators.

The fortunes of the Medici Bank lay close to the heart of their power. This was the foundation on which the authority of the family rested. Not only did it give them wide influence within the city (many businesses were founded on loans from the Medici Bank) but it also had branches all over Europe, in Venice and Rome, Lyons and London. John Hale suggests that Cosimo de' Medici was probably the wealthiest man in Europe.[16] Cosimo gave careful attention to the affairs of the bank and kept a close eye on the activities of each branch. Lorenzo, by contrast, neglected it. It bored him and he gave control to a general manager who failed to stop branches making unwise loans. In England, for example, the bank lent money to the losing side in the Wars of the Roses. By the time of Lorenzo's death in 1492 all branches outside Florence had closed and the Medici's financial power base had gone.

When the French invaded Italy in 1494 the Medici fell from power and this revealed the inherent instability of the constitution (see page 88). The power vacuum was filled first by a Dominican friar, Savonarola, then by a half-hearted attempt to restructure the constitution on Venetian lines (see pages 62 and 93). In 1512, papal troops captured Florence and the Medici were restored; a year later Lorenzo's son was elected Pope Leo X and for 15 years the city was effectively ruled from Rome. Apart from a brief revival from 1527-30, the Republic was dead and the Medici became dukes of Florence in 1537. The 'rise of the *signori*' had claimed its greatest victim.

5 Conclusion

Historians examine evidence and then construct patterns to explain it. The danger they face is the temptation to distort the facts to fit the pattern, or to select only that evidence which supports their argument. In the politics and government of Renaissance Italy there are two clear patterns. One is the transition to a more efficient modern bureaucracy with a centralised administrative structure. The other is the move from republican communes to the princely rule of a leading family. These are important themes we must be aware of. But we must also remember that not everything fits into those patterns. Genoa, for example, remained a weak republic that was faction-ridden, unstable and administratively chaotic. Milan evolved as a modern bureaucratic state, but Naples did not. Unlike most other states, the Republic of Venice did not change its constitution at all in this period, though the myth of Venice, as the stable and just republic, hid a more complex reality. But Venice did succeed in avoiding the factions into which so many other states degenerated. In Chapter two we saw that the family, not the commune commanded the primary allegiance of most people. This weakened the state and gave rise to the fear of faction. Florence's constitution was constructed around this fear, but despite this a single family, the Medici, came to dominate the Republic in the fifteenth century and returned as *signori* in the sixteenth. Although communes grew in strength in the Renaissance, it was ironic that in most states this process led ultimately to the political domination of a single family. In the princely states too, individual families remained powerful; the family of the prince may have been dominant, yet it still had to contend with many slightly weaker but still proud rivals. Renaissance states remained alliances of powerful families whether the form of government was republic or princedom; the social bonds of family were ultimately more powerful than the political ones of government.

References

1 Stanley Chojnacki, 'In Search of the Venetian Patriciate', in J.R. Hale (ed.), *Renaissance Venice* (Faber, 1973), p. 63.
2 Marin Sanudo in Finlay, *Venice*, p. 39.
3 Shakespeare, *Othello, the Moor of Venice* I. 3. 76.
4 Finlay, *Venice*, p. 39.
5 Chambers and Pullan, *Venice*, p. 45.
6 *Ibid*, pp. 55-6.
7 Guido Ruggiero, *Violence in Early Renaissance Venice* (Rutgers University Press, 1980), pp. 4-5.
8 Franco Gaeta and Gina Fasoli. See Finlay, *Venice*, pp. 27-37.
9 Machiavelli, *The Prince* (Penguin Books, 1961), pp. 101-2.
10 F. Guicciardini, *La Storia d'Italia*, ed. A Gherardi (Sansoni, Florence, 1919), Vol. 1, p. 64, author's translation.

11 John Hale, *Florence and the Medici: The Pattern of Control* (Thames and Hudson, 1977), pp. 16-17.

12 L.C. Gabel (ed.), *Memoirs of a Renaissance Pope: The Commentaries of Pius II* (Allen & Unwin, 1959), pp. 107-8.

13 Machiavelli, *Florentine History* (Dent, 1909), p. 278.

14 Vespasiano, *Princes, Popes, and Prelates*, p. 225.

15 N. Rubinstein, *The Government of Florence under the Medici 1434- 1494* (Oxford University Press, 1966), p. 129.

16 Hale, *Florence and the Medici*, p. 12.

Summary Diagram
The Political Structure

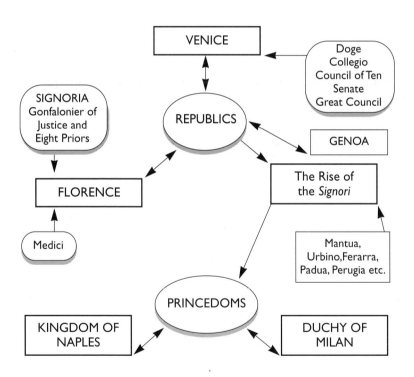

When you have read this chapter, find some of your fellow students who are studying Politics and Government and try to explain to them, in your own words, the main ideas you have learned here. Encourage them to ask you questions about it, and think about how these could be answered.

Answering source-based questions on 'The Political Structure'

1. *Three views of Cosimo de' Medici*

Read the extracts from Pius II, Machiavelli and Vespasiano, pages 47-8, then answer the following questions.

a) Machiavelli and Vespasiano both had reason to flatter the Medici, Pius II did not. How far is this fact reflected in their comments on Cosimo? How do they nevertheless hint at a darker side? (6 marks)

b) Machiavelli and Vespasiano were Florentines, Pius II was from Siena. How is this fact reflected in these comments? (4 marks)

c) Assess the value to the historian of these extracts and Cosimo's own comment on page 48. What picture of Cosimo emerges? (10 marks)

In assessing the value of contemporary descriptions of individuals, the sort of questions the historian needs to ask is fairly obvious. Had the author ever met his subject? Were they from the same city or did they meet in a 'foreign' context? Were they socially and politically equal or subservient to their subject? Were they well disposed and supportive, or hostile and critical? How independent were they when writing, and were they writing for publication or privately?

Answering essay questions on 'The Political Structure'

1. 'Although they were both republics, the governments of Florence and Venice were very different.' Discuss.

2. Why, and with what degree of justice, was the Venetian constitution so widely admired in Renaissance Italy?

3. To what extent can the Medici be regarded as the *signori* of Florence between 1434 and 1494?

4. How did the organisation of political power in either Florence or Venice reflect the economic and social structure of the city?

Questions on government and constitutions usually concentrate on the two republics of Venice and Florence. They may be treated separately, or they may be compared, as in question 1. Often the constitutional arrangements outlined in this chapter are related to economic and social issues, as in question 4. Both questions 2 and 3 require you to set a republic into the wider context of government in the rest of Italy.

In question 2 you need to say that so many Italian states admired what they perceived to be the stability of Venice because their own constitutions were unstable. Although many people, in theory, preferred republican government to a princedom, in practice they found it impossible to maintain a stable republic. Venice appeared to be free of the faction which crippled so many other states. Most of question 2, perhaps as much as 90 per cent, will be about Venice, but you cannot answer the question properly without that ten per cent which shows that other states admired what they themselves lacked. You need to discuss the structure of Venetian government - Doge, Collegio, Senate, Great Council, and the Council of Ten - but be sure this does not become just a description. *Use* that information to answer the question. Other states admired Venice for what appeared to be stability, justice and a balanced constitution: show how the monarchical position of a doge was restricted by the aristocratic power of the senate, which in turn was chosen by the 'democratic' power of the great council; show how executive and legislature shared power; show how lottery and election both played a part in choosing senators and doges. In the other part of the question, 'with what degree of justice', you need to examine the 'myth'. Was Venice as stable and just as other states believed? Was it the constitution which made it so, rather than the economy or its geographical position, or even the activities of the Council of Ten?

In question 3 you need to set your analysis of the Florentine constitution and the role of the Medici family within it, into the wider context of the 'rise of the *signori*' in so many of the other city states. Again, Florence may account for 90 per cent of your answer, but the 10 per cent on the other states is essential to answer the question.

By now, you should have read enough of this book (and, it is to be hoped, of others) to have some understanding as well as knowledge and to be able to use this information to answer the questions. The essay questions suggested above ask you to demonstrate your knowledge of the Florentine and Venetian constitutions, but they also require the understanding which comes from seeing those constitutions in two critical contexts. The first is the context of the wider history of the city, its economy and social structure. The second is the context of the other Italian states. That wider understanding should allow you to use the information you have to answer the questions.

5 Religion and the Church

1 The Structure and Condition of the Church

Giovanni de' Medici, the second son of Lorenzo the Magnificent, was elected Pope in 1513 and took the title Leo X. At the age of only 38, he was spectacularly young; at his death in 1521 he was, at 46, still eight years younger than most popes were at their election. 'Since God has given us the papacy', he was alleged to have told the Venetian ambassador, 'let us enjoy it'. Leo spent the wealth of the Church on composers and singers, scholars and poets, painters and architects. He indulged his pleasure in music, hunting and eating, but it was his misfortune to have to deal with the problem of Martin Luther. An institution like the Catholic Church needed reformation every few years. Many of the major reformers, like Francis of Assisi and Catherine of Siena, became saints because they reformed the administrative or moral abuses of the Church but defended its theology; they changed how it behaved, not what it believed. Luther and his fellow Protestants were fundamentally different, attacking not only the evident corruptions and shortcomings of the Church, but also its teaching and faith. The latter forms part of a theological debate on the nature of the Church, which belongs in a book on the Protestant reformation. Our concern here is with the ways in which the Church fell short of its own ideals.

The structure of the Church was complex; there were a number of different strands which ran through it. One important strand was hierarchical. The pope was the head of the universal Church. That Church was divided into provinces which were governed by archbishops. Provinces were divided into dioceses which were administered by bishops. Dioceses were divided into parishes which were served by priests. Outside this hierarchy were the Sacred College of Cardinals and the Curia. The cardinals were appointed for life by the pope and might be consulted by him when important decisions had to be made. But the pope was not obliged either to ask or to take his cardinals' advice. The Sacred College came into its own when a pope died, for it was the cardinals alone who elected the new pope. Their numbers grew: 12 cardinals elected Eugenius IV in 1431, 18 Pius II in 1458, 23 Alexander VI in 1492 and 38 Julius II in 1503. The Curia was the central bureaucracy of the Church, the civil service which administered the whole of western Christendom from Rome - or wherever the pope happened to be.

Another fundamental distinction in the Church was that between seculars and regulars. Regulars were those who belonged to one of the religious orders of monks, friars or nuns. They were governed by the 'rule' (*regula* in Latin) of the order which is why they were called regulars; they were also known as 'the religious'. To say that a man was a religious, or a regular, was another way of saying he was a monk or a friar. All the members of religious orders took oaths of poverty, chastity and obedience but each order was governed by a different rule. Monks lived enclosed lives in communities and were devoted to worship, scholarship and contemplation. Friars were mendicants who lived off alms and went out into the world begging and teaching. There were four main orders of Friars, of whom the best known were the Dominicans and the Franciscans. Until the twelfth century the Benedictines were the only monastic order in the Catholic Church, but from then on orders proliferated and by the Renaissance there were a large number. All clergy who were not members of religious orders were called seculars.

Abuse was widespread but not universal; Protestant historians have exaggerated the degree of corruption. Episcopal visitations - inspections by the bishops - revealed some low standards: in Bologna were crumbling, dilapidated churches and priests unable to identify the seven deadly sins or read the breviary (the book containing the psalms, prayers and readings of the Daily Office which every priest had to say); in Tuscany there was evidence of some abandoned churches, absentee clergy and villages with no services where marriages and burials took place without a priest; in Pisa there was absenteeism and pluralism; in Piacenza, sluttish conformism and a climate of general depression. The strict rules of the Church defining who could be ordained a priest, especially those regarding age and education, were too often ignored. Boys who had learned the mass by heart while acting as altar boys, but whose ability to read was very limited, were being ordained by bishops who had no personal knowledge of them. It was difficult to maintain high standards when entry to the priesthood was so easy. In one part of the papal states over 60 per cent of the laity had never received communion and few knew how to make the sign of the cross.

In the religious orders as well there were signs of decline. There was an abundance of houses but small numbers; instead of a community, many houses contained only one or two monks. Some monks and friars slept in separate rooms rather than a common dormitory, others wore linen underwear or ate more richly than their rule allowed. Filippino Lippi (see cover illustration) was the son of a monk and a novice nun. Far from being centres of scholarship and learning, many houses contained monks who were ignorant and even illiterate. Two Venetian monks in 1513 alleged that 'in the whole multitude of the religious, scarcely two in a hundred, or perhaps ten in a thousand, can be found who can read the daily services'.[1] That was probably an exaggeration, but the picture which emerges is of a lazy, tired and run-down Church. In Denys Hay's words, one finds not wickedness 'but torpor, tiny numbers and minor corruption'.[2]

The higher clergy were also in need of reform. The problem with bishops in the Italian Church was that there were so many of them.

Whereas England in 1400 was divided into 17 dioceses each with a bishop, Italy had 263. About 25 of these were wealthy and important, often centred on a large city. But the vast majority of dioceses were small and poor. Bishops would sometimes 'swap' dioceses and supplement that exchange with a money payment if they were moving from a poor see to a wealthy one. This led them to regard their office as property which could be bought and sold. Often a family would dominate a diocese for generations with successive members of the same house acting as bishop.

Reform of the Curia was high on the radicals' agenda. The Curia grew in size from about 500 men in 1378 to 2,000 in 1514. Some of these new offices were created just to sell, but the growth of the Curia was mostly concerned with the expansion in the administration of papal finances. Appointments to a wealthy benefice anywhere in the Church was handled by the Curia; they passed through many stages and at each stage money changed hands. It is true that Church officials were expected to live off their fees, and that such corruption was common in the administration of secular states, but still, the Church was not setting a good example. As a recent historian pointed out, 'the ecclesiastical system, at its administrative centre and at the grass-roots was stamped with the image of a commercial empire. The spirit of gain was more prominent than the gaining of spirits.'[3]

We must not allow the undoubted shortcomings of the Church to blind us to its merits and popular vitality. Records like visitation reports, Church court cases and the critical polemics of reformers, by their very nature, stress the faults not the virtues of the Renaissance Church. Religious processions were extremely popular; city crowds flocked to hear sermons and the educated bought printed copies of them; there were popular cults of the Blessed Virgin Mary and the Agnus Dei with its symbol of the Lamb and Flag. Prophecies and stories of miracles excited the public imagination and the painting and music of the age became integral to worship. Just as many parts of the Church were tired and decrepit, so others were lively and creative.

2 Popes, Councils and the Reform of the Church

The Catholic Church eventually reformed itself at the Council of Trent in 1545-63, but it had had the opportunity to do so a century and a half earlier. From 1409 to 1449 a series of General Councils of the Church were summoned to deal with three tasks: reuniting the Church, crushing the heresy of John Hus in Bohemia and reforming the Church. They succeeded in the first two but failed in the third and that failure paved the way for Luther and the Protestant reformation.

The Church needed re-uniting in 1409 because by then it had acquired two rival popes. From 1309 to 1377 the papacy had been based not in Rome but at Avignon, which today is part of France but was then ruled by the Angevin princes of Naples. On six occasions the cardinals elected Frenchmen as popes and the papal court remained at Avignon. But in 1378 Gregory XI died whilst in Rome and, under pressure from the city authorities and the Roman people, the cardinals immediately elected an Italian Archbishop as Pope Urban VI. Of the 16 cardinals 11 were French and five months later, claiming the first election had been invalid because they were being coerced by a hostile mob, they proceeded to a second election, and so the Church had two popes. This was known as the Great Schism. In 1409 a Council of the Church met at Pisa to resolve the problem. It deposed both popes and elected a new one to replace them. But neither pope accepted his deposition and after the Council of Pisa the Church found itself not with two popes but with three. Each of the three popes appointed his own cardinals, and as a pope died, so his cardinals would elect a successor, thus creating three dynasties of popes. By 1414 the three rival Popes were Gregory XII, Benedict XIII and John XXIII.

General Councils were meetings of the cardinals, archbishops and bishops of the Church, together with representatives of the lower clergy from all over Christendom. They were recognised as having great authority; the early ones like the Council of Nicaea in AD 325 had established the fundamental creeds of the faith. In theory, a General Council could depose a pope for heresy, but a council could be legitimately summoned only by a pope. Some theologians, most notably those at the University of Paris, argued that General Councils were superior to popes and advocated the summoning of a General Council which would seek not only to heal the schism but also to reform the Church. Despite the failure at Pisa, another council met at Constance in 1414. Over 600 men attended the Council but their entourages meant that many thousands crowded into the small Swiss city. As well as 29 cardinals, 33 archbishops and 150 bishops there were also many doctors of the Church and representatives of the lower clergy. Where Pisa had rushed headlong into the deposition of popes, Constance moved with considerable care and diplomacy. The political ground was prepared and each of the popes was isolated. The Holy Roman Emperor, Sigismund, attended some sessions of the Council in person and Henry V of England was represented by his uncle, Cardinal Beaufort. It took the council three years of careful negotiation, and it was not until July 1417 that all three popes had successfully been deposed.

What was to happen next was of critical importance. The radicals in the council wanted to reform the Church before a new pope was elected. This would have allowed the council to introduce major reforms in the central administration of the Church, the Curia, and to address the critical question of Church finances, without a pope, who had a vested interest in the matter, to restrain them. The conservatives, however, wanted to proceed immediately to the election of a new pope and to leave the question of Church reform up to him. Some cardinals were reformers, but most took a conservative line. The strongest desire to curb the power of the papacy came from the bishops, but many of the lower clergy resisted moves which would have given their bishops more power. Ultimately, however, it was national politics which decided the issue. In September the English delegates switched from the reforming to the conservative side and on 11 November 1417 Martin V was elected Pope of a re-united Church. This tolled the death knell for radical reform. In October 1417 the Council of Constance had passed one decree, *Frequente*, which said that councils must meet regularly, whether the pope wanted one or not. But otherwise, the reform of the Church was left to the new Pope. If Martin V had been a great reforming Pope the Protestant schism of the sixteenth century might have been averted, but he was not. His reforms were minor and cosmetic. He saw the whole conciliar movement as a threat to the power of the papacy and skilfully undermined it.

The Council of Constance united the Church but failed either to reform it or to deal effectually with the Bohemian heretics. Another council met at Basle in 1431. The Hussite movement was effectively crushed and the Council took the credit for this. But the reform of the Church was now openly and actively opposed by the papacy. A reforming group of radical lower clergy dominated the council and a serious split developed which culminated in an unseemly brawl in Basle cathedral in May 1437. The Pope, Eugenius IV, ordered the council to transfer to Ferrara, but the radicals refused to go with the majority and a rump remained at Basle. The Council of Ferrara soon moved to Florence as a larger city was needed and the Pope was resident in the city until 1443. The purpose of this council was to meet delegates from the eastern, Greek, Orthodox Church in the hope of re-uniting the whole of Christendom. The presence of a large number of Greek churchmen and scholars in the city gave a great boost to the study of Greek amongst Florentine scholars. The negotiations led in 1439 to a decree of union between the Latin and Greek Churches. However, the delegates had exceeded their authority and the agreement was repudiated by the Orthodox Church in Constantinople and so came to nothing. Meanwhile at Basle the radicals continued to meet until 1449, passing reforming decrees which were not recognised by the Church. The conciliar attempt to reform the Church had failed.

3 The Renaissance Papacy

The Renaissance popes were a varied bunch. It is difficult to find an adjective which can describe them collectively. Not all were glittering, nor all corrupt; not all were scholarly, nor all self-seeking; few were thoroughly wicked and even fewer saintly. From the election of Martin V in 1417 to the return to the Vatican in 1530 of Clement VII after the Sack of Rome (1527), 14 men sat upon the throne of St Peter. Two were from great Roman families, two Venetian, two Medici from Florence, two Borgias from Spain, two Piccolomini from Siena, one was Dutch.

The Renaissance Popes 1417-1534			
Martin V	1417-31	Colonna Family	Rome
Eugenius IV	1431-47	Condulmer Family	Venice
Nicholas V	1447-55	Parentucelli Family	Sarzana
Calixtus III	1455-58	Borgia Family	Spain
Pius II	1458-64	Piccolomini Family	Siena
Paul II	1464-71	Barbo Family	Venice
Sixtus IV	1471-84	della Rovere Family	Savona
Innocent VIII	1484-92	Cibo Family	Genoa
Alexander VI	1492-1503	Borgia Family	Spain
Pius III	1503*	Piccolomini Family	Siena
Julius II	1503-13	della Rovere Family	Savona
Leo X	1513-21	Medici Family	Florence
Adrian VI	1522-23	Dedel Family	Utrecht
Clement VII	1523-34	Medici Family	Florence

* Elected 22 September, died 18 October 1503

It was expected that, once elected pope, a man would benefit his family and his home city. When Aeneus Sylvius Piccolomini became Pope Pius II in 1458 he had two nephews; one, a soldier, was soon in part command of the papal army, the other, a churchman, although only 21, was appointed Archbishop of Siena and cardinal, and eventually became Pope himself as Pius III. No-one considered this corrupt; it would have been unnatural for Pius II to have done otherwise. The Pope's home city of Siena was equally favoured. It was made an archdiocese; the papal court was based there for eight months, thus bringing great wealth to the city; and Catherine of Siena, the fourteenth-century mystic, was canonised.

If not a saint, Pius II was a scholar of sorts and his long and rambling memoirs reveal a well-intentioned man. Rodrigo Borgia, who became Pope Alexander VI in 1492, was equally determined to advance his family but his ruthless manner and the fact that his family consisted of his own children rather than nephews has resulted in less favourable treatment from historians. Michael Mallett's splendid study of the family has flushed away the old nonsense about their being incestuous poisoners. Alexander's daughter Lucrezia, far from having sex with her father and brother, appears as a tragic, almost noble, figure who was used to further the family fortunes in unhappy dynastic marriages. Her brother Cesare, a scholar, a soldier and a skilful politician, was undoubtedly a cruel and ruthless man, well able to murder the only husband his sister really loved, when he believed that he threatened his safety. But Mallett has shown that it was Alexander, not Cesare, who was in control. Although he lacked the spirituality one might expect in a pope, Alexander VI had all the qualities which would be admired in a great secular ruler. Sigismondo de' Conti, who worked in the Curia, wrote 'this Pope, if he had not had children and so much affection for them would have left a better memory of himself'.[4] Many popes had children. Even Pius II fathered two, who died in infancy, but that was before he became a priest. Alexander's children were born well before he became Pope, most within a long-term liaison with a highly respectable woman. Such things were not uncommon and were tolerated. What did scandalise contemporaries was Alexander's affair with the 20-year-old aristocratic beauty Guilia Farnese, after he had been elected Pope and, even more, the rumours surrounding the parentage of the *Infans Romanus*, Giovanni Borgia, born in the Vatican in 1498. Far more significant than these sexual peccadilloes, however, was the political question of whether family interests were put before the well-being of the papacy and the Church when deciding diplomatic policy.

The Borgias were a Spanish family with no territorial homeland in Italy. The Pope worked to carve a Borgia province for his son Cesare out of the papal states and to make him Duke of Romagna. Certainly, Alexander used papal resources and papal diplomacy to further his family aim of establishing a Borgia state. Two campaigns were fought in the Romagna and another further south in the papal states which established Cesare as Duke. But such a policy was consistent with the traditional papal aim of keeping the States of the Church under their command. Time after time the papal vicars who ruled the states would establish independence and then popes would fight a campaign to re-establish control. Alexander's policy in the Romagna had a dual aim; family ambition did not seriously conflict with the interests of the papacy and when it did, as in the Spring of 1503, Alexander resisted Cesare's advice and put papacy before family. The crucial question for the Borgia family was whether Cesare would be able to remain Duke of Romagna after his father's death. He planned to dominate the next papal election to ensure the cardinals chose a candidate who favoured him. But in the hot summer of 1503 both Alexander and Cesare caught malaria. It killed the Pope and although Cesare survived, he was too ill to prevent the eventual election of Cardinal Giuliano della Rovere, the greatest enemy of the Borgias, as Pope Julius II.

Julius II (1503-13) was the greatest warrior amongst the Renaissance popes. The della Rovere family had been an obscure one before his uncle became Pope in 1471. Within four months of that election, the papal nephew was made a cardinal at the age of 28. Giuliano was not the only relative of the new Pope's to be advanced, but he was the outstanding one and soon became a dominant force in the Sacred College. As Pope, he introduced financial and administrative reforms and showed his warrior's prowess in re-establishing control over the papal states. He persuaded Michelangelo, a sculptor, to paint the ceiling of the Sistine Chapel, the pope's private chapel in the Vatican named after his uncle Pope Sixtus IV (1471-84) who built it; he employed Raphael to decorate the Vatican palace, and it was for Pope Julius that *The School of Athens* was painted (see the illustrations on pages 115 and 119). He commissioned a huge and elaborate tomb for himself from Michelangelo, an undertaking so over-ambitious it was never completed. Like Alexander VI, he would have made a great secular leader, but he lacked the spiritual qualities needed in a pope. Christine Shaw, his recent biographer, who says he should have been a soldier, describes him as a 'plain-spoken, short-tempered, vigorous, impetuous, big-hearted man of action', but concedes 'he was really not cut out to be a pope'.[5]

We must not allow the worldly splendour of Alexander VI, Julius II and Leo X to blind us to the fact that some Renaissance popes brought more spiritual and intellectual qualities to the papacy. If Julius II was better suited to be a soldier, then the pious Eugenius IV (1431-47) would have made a better monk. The problem was that a successful pope needed both worldly and spiritual qualities which were rarely combined in a single man, and the cardinals recognised this. Writing of the election of Alexander VI, Michael Mallett reflects:

1   in 1492 a realisation both of the increasingly secular nature of the
    Papacy itself, and also of the seriousness of the political situation of the
    time, led the cardinals to abandon the more saintly candidates and
    choose a man who was noted for his administrative abilities and his
5   political acumen rather than for his saintliness.[6]

4 Christianity and the Renaissance

Burckhardt implied, and some of his less cautious followers asserted, that there was in the Renaissance a pagan strand. Denys Hay speaks for modern scholars when he insists, 'no one can any longer accept unquestioningly the existence of that paganism ... and no one can regard humanist writing as atheistical'.[7] It is true that Renaissance scholars studied the pagan writers of the Ancient World and an increasing number of artists illustrated classical themes. However, studies of the active élite, whose works of scholarship, literature and art were at the heart of the Renaissance, have shown that in no way can they be described as pagan. But was that how they were seen by clergy and laity outside that élite? Was the Church as a whole hostile to the Renaissance?

The answer to this question is complex. There was an anti-intellectual faction in the Church which argued that too much study and learning could distract people from living the holy life and devoting themselves to piety and good works. To them, the emphasis on pagan literature seemed an unnecessary distraction. But there were plenty in the Church to argue against them, insisting that knowledge was light and poetry a way to understand divine truth. Some sermons of the day reflected the new learning. St Antonino, who was Archbishop of Florence from 1446 to 1459, was suspicious of poetry and fables, but a friend to many of the classical scholars. The Church contained both critics and advocates of the new learning.

a) Girolamo Savonarola 1452-98: A Critic

Variously described as theologian, preacher, prophet, heretic and martyr, Savonarola became Prior of S. Marco, the house of Dominican friars in Florence, in 1491. As a revivalist preacher he was a charismatic figure. His powerful sermons had an emotional effect on his huge congregations and he used them to call for a moral reformation in the city. He also indulged in prophecy, foretelling destruction for Florence if it did not abandon its sinful ways. His prediction that 'soon the deluge will come - that is, soldiers and princes who would take the cities and fortresses by merely presenting themselves before the walls' was interpreted (after the event) as having been a reference to the French invasion of 1494.[8] He followed a great tradition of prophecy in the city and it has been argued that Florence affected Savonarola as much as Savonarola affected Florence.[9] He was a complicated figure, and the reaction of Florentines to him was equally complex. He was a critic of the Medici, first on moral grounds and later on political ones, but still Lorenzo summoned Savonarola to attend him as he was dying.

Two years after Lorenzo's death, the invading French army swept through Italy and Piero de' Medici mishandled the crisis so completely he was driven from authority (see pages 87-9). The power-vacuum that was left was filled by Savonarola. He never held any political office but for four years, from 1494 to 1498, he ruled Florence from the pulpit. Time and again, the elections to the *signoria* produced a majority of his supporters who followed his guidance in their conduct of the affairs of the city. Savonarola encouraged two reform movements, one moral and the other constitutional. Politically, he set out to turn Florence into a true republic, restructuring its constitution to make it more like that of Venice. Morally, he raged against gambling, drinking, dancing, indecent carnival songs, and a range of sexual indulgences - most of all sodomy for which the city was notorious. He denounced the elaborate fashions of the day, especially those designed to draw attention to female breasts and male genitals. He encouraged children, through the youth organisations he set up, to report on their parents' moral failings. After four years, Savonarola fell from power and was burned in a public execution in the *Piazza della Signoria* (see the illustration below). Florence had been divided into a number of factions and his fall came when the group who supported him, the *piagnoni* (snivellers), no longer had a majority on the *signoria*. After four years, most Florentines were tired of the rigours of moral reform and disturbed by the friar, who, pushed on by his more extreme followers, adopted more and more uncompromising positions. But the main reason for his fall was his foreign policy and the hostility to him of the papacy. He was condemned by the Borgia Pope, Alexander VI, who excommunicated him for heresy, not because of his denunciation of papal morals, but because he alone continued to support the French when the Pope was building an alliance to drive them out of Italy.

Savonarola was, perhaps, most notorious for the 'bonfires of vanities' he encouraged, but these should not be misunderstood. He did not invent them; they were already a common way of showing public contrition. In 1497, on the day before Lent began, when Carnival was

Anon: Execution of Savonarola, *Museo S. Marco, Florence. This shows the Piazza della Signoria in 1498. Florence Cathedral is on the far left, the palace of the signoria with its bell tower is centre right. The square tower, just right of the Cathedral, is the Bargello where the Law Officers were based. The artist has painted the piazza with geometrical paving stones to show off his mastery of the technique of perspective*

usually celebrated, he set fire to a great wooden pyramid piled high with 'vanities' acquired by his boys in a house-to-house collection - 'obscene books and pictures, lutes, women's false hair, cosmetics, perfumes, mirrors, dolls, playing cards, dice, gaming tables'.[10] Although these included 'indecent drawings', it is wrong to suggest that this was some philistine burning of books and fine paintings; Savonarola's opposition to Renaissance ideas was more complex and subtle. He had no objection to art and learning provided it was used to serve Christian purposes by encouraging devotion and meditation, rather than exploring the pagan philosophy of the Ancient World. But he was out of sympathy with the new attitude of the humanist scholars to the pagan writings of the Greeks and Romans (see Chapter six), which he regarded as being incompatible with the calling of a Christian.

b) Clerical Advocates of the New Learning

Just as in society only an élite was affected by Renaissance ideas, so in the Church most were uninterested and indifferent. As so many of the lower clergy were ill-educated and ignorant, it is little surprise that most were unaffected by, even unaware of, the revival of interest in classical civilisation. The bishops were little better. Perhaps a quarter of them were well educated, but most of these were lawyers and out of a sample of 126 whom Hay examined only two were significant intellectual figures, and both of these went on to be cardinals. Peter Burke's list of 600 élite figures includes 78 clergy, of whom only 44 were writers.[11]

Although few in numbers, there were amongst the cardinals and the popes some important patrons and even a few scholars. Pope Pius II had a humanist training. Before he became Pope, he wrote a novel and a comic play, satires and an historical treatise. As Pope he wrote his memoirs and continued to practise the art of oratory of which he believed himself to be a master. He also saw himself as a patron of builders, scholars and artists, but the extent of his patronage, just as his reputation as 'the humanist Pope', has been exaggerated. More significant was his friend and one-time patron, Pope Nicholas V (1447-55). He was a scholar who surrounded himself with writers and men of learning, a friend of Cosimo de' Medici and some of the leading Florentine humanists. He loved books and established the foundations of the Vatican Library. He collected 1,200 Greek and Latin works, all of which were in manuscript form as the art of printing was not yet established. He employed men not only to copy books by hand, but also to translate Greek works into Latin, so that they were more widely accessible. He engaged architects and builders to construct churches, palaces, bridges and fortifications, and painters to decorate his buildings. He reconstructed the ancient Capitol in Rome, and was Pope in the fateful year when

Constantinople fell to the Turks. The Florentine bookseller Vespasiano, of whom he was a customer, described him as 'the ornament and the light of literature and of learned men'.[12] Vespasiano's compliment was, for once, deserved - but there were few popes or other churchmen for whom the same could be said.

One of the major preoccupations of the Renaissance mind was to reconcile apparent opposites into a state of balance - soldiers and scholars, the active and the contemplative, the Christian and the classical (see page 125-7). This did not mean that humanists saw Christianity and paganism as being equal. The two were to be reconciled within a Christian universe. Michelangelo was a devout Catholic, yet on the ceiling of the Sistine Chapel he placed alternately Old Testament prophets and Roman sibyls - the prophetesses of the pagan world (see the illustration on page 119). But he brought the two realms together in order to proclaim the Christian message of redemption. To understand how he was able to do this we need first to examine the Renaissance exploration of classical learning and the way this was interpreted by the artists.

5 Conclusion

It is difficult for English people today to view the Renaissance Church with much degree of sympathetic insight. Atheists and agnostics find its most passionately held beliefs unreasonable. Protestants, eager to defend their 'reformation', recognise its shortcomings, but do not value what contemporaries regarded as its strengths. Even modern Catholics are disinclined to defend an unreformed Church with which they increasingly have less and less in common. And yet in Renaissance Italy, the Church occupied a central position and almost everyone regarded themselves as a member of it. It is not the historian's task to judge the practices of the past by the standards of the present; rather he or she must seek to understand and enter into the minds of people who thought very differently from most of us.

The Church believed that whenever a priest celebrated mass, the bread and wine really became the body and blood of Christ. Only a priest could celebrate this awesome sacrament and the miraculous change occurred whether or not he was a good man. Even an unworthy priest could bring God to the people; an unworthy Church could intercede between God and man. Outside of the Church there was no salvation; individual men and women did not have a 'direct line' to Heaven, but could come to God only through the Church, regardless of its state of health at the time. This did not mean that people did not care if the Church was corrupt; Catholic reformers raged about it - indeed, it was often said that all good Catholics were anti-clerical. But that unworthiness did not invalidate the Church's exercise of its spiritual functions. The pope was the successor of St Peter, whose authority he inherited, whether he was a saint or (more likely) a sinner.

The remarkable worldly success of the Church, in the millennium before the Renaissance, added to its problems. It was far easier for the Church to maintain a spiritual purity when it was a persecuted minority sect in the Roman Empire. In the Christian states which grew out of the ruins of that Empire, the Church supported the state and the state the Church. Archbishops crowned kings and kings sought the advice and counsel of the leaders of the Church. Moreover, when the papacy acquired the overlordship of the papal states, the pope became a temporal ruler as well as a spiritual leader. Everywhere, the Church appeared to be supporting the rulers of states rather than the subjects. It held out the promise of heaven as a future reward to the poor and urged them to obedience and acceptance of their wretched lot on earth; religion became an agency of social control. Of course, there were many contemporary critics within the Church who condemned this, but in general people accepted the Church as it was, recognised it was unworthy, but still acknowledged its authority. However hard it may be, we must put aside judgement; rather than condemning, we must seek to understand Leo X, Julius II and Alexander VI, for, unless we can comprehend the Renaissance papacy and accept the attitudes of people towards it, we shall never understand Renaissance Italy.

References
1   Denys Hay, *The Church in Italy in the Fifteenth Century* (Cambridge University Press, 1977), p. 63.
2   *Ibid*, p. 59.
3   C.M.D. Crowder, *Unity, Heresy and Reform, 1378-1460* (Arnold, 1977), p. 21.
4   Michael Mallett, *The Borgias: The Rise and Fall of a Renaissance Dynasty* (Bodley Head, 1969), p. 255.
5   Christine Shaw, *Julius II: The Warrior Pope* (Blackwell, 1993), p. 315.
6   Mallett, *Borgias,* p. 118.
7   Hay, *Church in Italy,* p. 92.
8   R. Ridolphi, *The Life of Girolamo Savonarola* (RKP, 1959), p. 72.
9   D. Weinstein, *Savonarola and Florence* (Princeton University Press, 1970).
10 Ridolphi, *Savonarola,* p. 184.
11 P. Burke, *Renaissance Italy 1420-1540* (Batsford, 1972), p. 62.
12 Vespasiano, *Princes, Popes and Prelates,* p. 51.

Summary Diagram
Religion and the Church

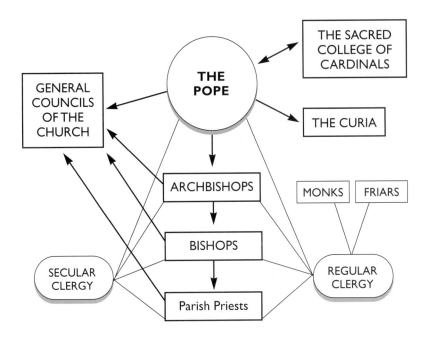

THE SACRED COLLEGE OF CARDINALS

GENERAL COUNCILS OF THE CHURCH

THE POPE

THE CURIA

ARCHBISHOPS

MONKS   FRIARS

BISHOPS

SECULAR CLERGY

REGULAR CLERGY

Parish Priests

Answering essay questions on 'Religion and the Church'

Most essay questions on religion will arise in connection with the matters discussed in Chapters six, seven and eight, when its concerns are related to intellectual and cultural aspects of the Renaissance. But there are one or two questions we can ask solely about religion.

1. 'A profoundly Christian age.' Discuss this view of Renaissance Italy.

2. Why did Savonarola dominate Florence for only four years?

Question 1 is a deliberately provocative question which invites you to discuss the cases for and against the statement. In many ways society was worldly and the Church corrupt and tired. You can discuss the characters of some of the Renaissance popes and the evidence of low religious standards of the secular and regular clergy and of the laity. The failure to reform the Church will form part of the case against the statement. On the other hand this was an age in which almost everyone was a Christian (albeit a bad one). There was an attempt to reform the Church. The Church was powerful and central in people's lives. Many artists were inspired by Christian subject matter. The complex reaction of the Church to the study of the Ancient World also needs to be discussed. But first, you need to consider what a 'Christian' age means; is it necessarily the same as a 'pious' age?

In question 2, although you also need to explain what you mean by 'dominate', the crucial word is 'only'. To answer the question properly you need to explain how the friar was able to dominate the city for four years, but no longer. It is useful, therefore, to explore what were the various foundations of his power and then to see how each of these in turn disappeared. Therefore, although the question is similar to 'why did Savonarola fall from power?' it is rather more complex and needs a wider-ranging discussion of the friar's power bases.

Some advice on writing Introductions and Conclusions
Before reading this section, you would find it useful to re-read the advice on planning an essay given in the Study Guide to Chapter three. The introduction to your essay needs to do at least two things: it should examine the question in detail and outline to the reader how you propose to answer it. People sometimes talk of 'unwrapping' the question. What they mean by this is taking it apart and seeing what it involves, finding out what other questions may be hidden inside it. For example, question 2, 'why did Savonarola dominate Florence for only four years?' has other questions hidden within. How did he dominate the city, and why use the word 'dominate' instead of 'rule'? What were the bases of his power in the city? How and why did he successfully dominate it for four years? What opposition was there to him? How and why did he fall from power after four years? You can use your introduction to discuss what the question involves and outline to your reader how you intend to answer it. Say what your paragraphs will be about and how they will address the question. Give the readers an idea of where you are taking them, so that they are aware of why the material you present them with later in the essay is relevant.

Your conclusion should draw everything together. If you have followed the advice on page 37 above, the final sentence of each paragraph will show its relevance to the question. So you will find it useful to read the final sentence of each paragraph before writing your conclusion. This should show how everything in the essay unites to provide a concise and precise answer to the question. Thus, the conclusion also has two main purposes. One is to draw the whole essay together and remind the reader of the major points you have established in each paragraph. The other is to summarise the answer to the question in as direct a way as you can.

6 The Ancient World and Renaissance Humanism

The last four chapters examined the economic, social, political and religious contexts in which the Renaissance took place. Now we return to the themes outlined in the first section of the introduction to this book, and you would do well to re-read that section before looking at the rest of this chapter. European history has been dominated by two major traditions: one was the classical civilisation of Greece and Rome; Christianity was the other. The Ancient World left behind it intellectual and cultural riches which posed a problem to Christians who had divergent values and viewed the world differently (see pages 95-7 and 125-7). Medieval Christendom struggled for many centuries with the problem of how to regard the Ancients and how to use their legacy. It was the voluminous commentaries on the works of Aristotle by the Italian theologian St Thomas Aquinas (c.1225-74) which eventually established the firm philosophical basis on which the Catholic Church in the Middle Ages defined its relationship to the Ancient World. Aquinas accepted many of Aristotle's arguments but adapted and extended them to meet the needs of a Christian society. Without challenging Aquinas's theology, the humanist scholars of the Renaissance set out to re-define the relationship between Christianity and classical civilisation. This chapter and, to some extent, the next examine this re-definition and consider how its study of the Ancient World of Greece and Rome affected Renaissance Italy.

1 The Latin Language and the Roman Republic

In the second section of this chapter we shall examine the study of Greek literature in the Renaissance; our concern here is with Roman civilisation and with Latin - for Italian scholars, their 'home' language. The study of the Latin language lay at the heart of the Italian Renaissance, but no literary manuscripts penned in the ancient period survived. Latin works reached the Renaissance by means of a series of handwritten copies made over the centuries, in the course of which the original text became corrupted. When the Roman Empire in the West fell, it was the monastic libraries that preserved and transmitted the Latin texts of Roman civilisation. Each time a manuscript was re-copied, in an age when pure classical Latin was no longer written, there was an additional opportunity for errors to creep in; so earlier copies were likely to have fewer inaccuracies. The Christian scribes, who copied classical texts in monastic libraries, also added glosses. These were words inserted between the lines or in the margin to explain a passage, or to add a Christian comment upon it. In subsequent copies these became incorporated into the text. Some works had been 'lost'. What this usually meant was that although copies survived in monastic libraries, they had been mislaid

or forgotten and, instead of still being regularly copied and distrib-
uted, they lay neglected on the shelves. So, some Latin texts of Roman
writers were known in the late Middle Ages in corrupt forms; others
had been lost. Renaissance humanist scholars set out to rectify this.
The search for accurate texts preoccupied the early humanists; in the
words of one, Niccolò Niccoli (1364-1437),

> until the ancient sources flow clear again, all efforts must be directed
> with single mindedness to the task of recovering the classical languages
> and the genuine readings of the ancient works.[1]

The Italian poet and scholar Petrarch (1304-74) found copies of
works by Cicero, the Roman orator, and Livy, the historian. He re-
discovered an important speech of Cicero's, and a number of his
letters in Verona; from French cathedral libraries, he recovered part
of the text of Livy's *History of Rome*. His contemporary Boccaccio
(1313-75) drew attention to the historical writings of Tacitus which
survived in the monastic library at Monte Cassino. Soon a number of
humanists were engaged in a widespread search for manuscripts in
libraries all over Europe. None travelled further or showed more
enthusiasm than Poggio Bracciolini (1380-1459). A secretary at the
papal court, Poggio accompanied the pope to the Council of
Constance and took the opportunity to search for manuscripts in the
libraries of Swiss monasteries, before going on to France, Germany
and England.

Once manuscripts had been found, philologists studied them. The
term 'philologist' means, in general 'one devoted to learning or literature, a classical scholar'; it also has a more particular meaning as 'a
person versed in the science of language, a linguistic scholar'.[2] The
first meaning describes all Renaissance humanists; the second only a
small minority of the best. One of the most skilled was Lorenzo Valla
(1407-57) whose knowledge of the Latin language and its development enabled him to date a document from its style. He recognised
anachronisms and could identify later additions to manuscripts and
remove them. In the *Donation of Constantine* (1440), he applied this
scholarship to the document in which the papacy believed the fourth
century Emperor Constantine had given it temporal power over the
papal states. Valla showed this to be an eighth century forgery. But
Valla was more than just a clever detective; his love for the Latin
language was close to the heart of humanism. The Roman Empire, he
pointed out, had faded away, but the language still lived:

> 1 The Roman dominion, the peoples and nations long ago threw off as an
> unwelcome burden; the language of Rome they have thought sweeter
> than any nectar, more splendid than any silk, more precious than any
> gold or gems, and they have embraced it as if it were a god sent from
> 5 Paradise. Great, therefore, is the sacramental power of the Latin
> language. We have lost Rome, we have lost authority, we have lost

dominion, yet we reign still, by this more splendid sovereignty, in a great part of the world. For wherever the Roman tongue holds sway, there is the Roman Empire.[3]

When the humanist scholars looked back to the history of Rome, what they really admired was the purity and honour of the Roman Republic (510-c.23 BC), rather than the gross excesses of the Roman Empire which followed it. Some humanists sought to inspire Renaissance cities with the civic virtue of the Roman Republic - the active participation of its leading citizens in government. Coluccio Salutati (1331-1406) held the office of Chancellor of Florence for the last 30 years of his life. Leonardo Bruni (1370-1444), his pupil and disciple, followed him as Chancellor of Florence in 1427. Both made important contributions to the development of Civic Humanism. At the time when Giangaleazzo Visconti of Milan was threatening the Florentine Republic (see page 43), Salutati's letters defended the city's liberty and Bruni's *Panegyric of the City of Florence* (1401) was a defence of Florentine republicanism and literary culture against Milanese despotism. In 1421, Bruni argued that the city should be defended by its own people in a citizen militia rather than by mercenaries and so established a theme reprised by Machiavelli and other later humanists again and again (see page 91).

So, the early humanists concentrated on the Latin writings of the Roman world; they searched libraries for lost works and more accurate copies of known ones; they studied the language in which they were written and the ideas they contained; they copied the style of the Latin writers - Cicero was universally considered the best and his work was widely imitated. They also discussed the ideas and values of the Roman world, especially its sense of civic pride. Unlike the medieval schoolmen who had 'Christianised' the Latin writers, Renaissance humanists sought to restore them to their pagan integrity and only then to consider what relevance their ideas had for a Christian, living in Renaissance Italy.

2 The Growth of Greek Studies 1394-1471

In May 1453, after a two month siege, the Ottoman sultan, Mehmet II, captured Constantinople and killed Constantine XIII, the last Emperor of what was still officially the eastern Roman Empire but is usually known, after the ancient name for the city, as the Byzantine Empire. The city of Constantinople was Greek in tradition, culture and learning. The three days of pillage which followed its fall saw the sparing of its architectural riches. Its other chief cultural treasures were its scholars and their manuscripts, some of whom found their way to Italy. The Byzantines were known as 'the librarians of the world'. Just as the major Latin texts were held in Italy and Western Europe, so the safekeeping of Greek literature rested largely with

Constantinople. It used to be argued that it was the arrival of Greek scholars and their manuscripts from Constantinople after 1453 that began the Greek phase of the Italian Renaissance. That is untrue. Certainly it gave it a new impetus and acceleration, but Greek studies were already well established in Italy by then.

Manuel Chrysoloras (1350-1415) was sent to Italy by the Byzantine Emperor to seek help against the Turks, and Coluccio Salutati, the Chancellor of Florence, persuaded the University of Florence to offer him the post of Professor of Greek. Chrysoloras taught there for three decisive years from 1397 to 1400, not only instructing his students in the Greek language, but also inspiring them with his boundless enthusiasm for Greek literature, thought and art. Leonardo Bruni abandoned his legal studies to learn Greek from Chrysoloras, telling himself,

> There are plenty of teachers of the Civil Law, so you will always be able to study that, but this is the one and only teacher of Greek; if he should disappear, there would then be nobody from whom you could learn Greek.[4]

Whereas all scholars could read and write Latin, only a minority ever learned Greek. Teachers of Greek needed grammars and lexicons (word lists or dictionaries) for their pupils to use. In practical terms Manuel Chrysoloras's Greek Grammar of 1398 was of paramount importance. It was improved by Guarino da Verona in 1417, who produced a Greek lexicon in 1440. Guarino (1374-1460) was an Italian who had studied in Constantinople and acquired not only an unrivalled knowledge of Greek but also a collection of manuscripts. He taught for four years at the University of Florence, building on the foundation Manuel Chrysoloras had laid. But it was at Ferrara that Guarino founded perhaps the greatest of Renaissance schools which he ran from 1429 until his death in 1460. He was a teacher of Greek rather than a philosopher or original thinker, but he and his pupils played a crucial role in establishing Greek as well as Latin as an important medium of scholarship.

Guarino acted as a translator when a delegation of Greek churchmen from Constantinople met the Roman Church at the Council of Florence in 1438-9 (see page 58). Although the council failed in its aim to reunite the eastern and the western Churches, it did encourage Greek learning in Italy. The Greek delegates brought copies of manuscripts with them and a few stayed in Italy. One who settled was Bessarion (1403-72) who converted to the Roman Church, became a Cardinal and was almost elected pope in 1455. He was a friend to the great Italian humanists and himself translated a number of Greek works into Latin, including some of Plato's dialogues. In 1468 he left his collection of Greek manuscripts to the library of St Mark in Venice reflecting that,

1   From almost the earliest years of my boyhood I strove with all my
might, main, effort and concentration to assemble as many books as I
could on every sort of subject. Not only did I copy many in my own
hand when I was a boy or youth, but I spent what I could set aside from
5   my small savings on buying books. For I could think of no more noble
or splendid possession, no treasure more useful or valuable, that I could
possibly gather for myself... Since then, all my strength, my effort, my
time, my capacity and my concentration has been devoted to seeking
out Greek books. For I feared - indeed I was consumed with terror -
10   lest all those wonderful books, the product of so much toil and study by
the greatest human minds, those very beacons to the earth, should be
brought to danger and destruction in an instant... So I assembled
almost all the works of the wise men of Greece, especially those which
were rare and difficult to find.[5]

Bessarion's library was a manuscript one, but it was the introduction
of printing to Italy in the final third of the fifteenth century that revo-
lutionised the distribution of texts and, by the creation of multiple
copies, ensured that works were never again lost. The printing press
reached Venice in 1469, and by the end of the century it was the most
important publishing centre not only in Italy, but in the whole of
Europe. Two Venetian presses were pre-eminent: the Giunti for quantity and profit, and the Aldine Press, founded by Aldus Manutius, for
quality and scholarship. Although Aldus never gained direct access to
the Bessarion manuscripts, his Greek first editions were a great
achievement. The high quality of his typefaces and book production
overcame much of the prejudice of conservative scholars against the
printed book. 'While he was selling scholarship to the printers with
one hand, with the other Aldus was selling printing to the scholars.'[6]
He, more than anyone, united in Venice the worlds of humanism and
of business.

3 The Florentine Neoplatonists

Of all the students of Greek in Renaissance Italy, the best-known are
the Neoplatonists who studied in and around Florence. Neoplatonism
was not simply a revival of the ideas of Plato. In the third century AD,
the Greek philosopher Plotinus created a synthesis of the collective
wisdom of the Greek world by incorporating into Platonism what he
regarded as the best of Aristotle, Pythagoras and other Greek philosophers; this synthesis was called Neoplatonism. Renaissance
Neoplatonists revived this classical Neoplatonism, and combined it
with Christianity and with a new awareness of the writings of Plato
himself.

a) Marsiglio Ficino 1433-99

Only a small proportion of Plato's works had been known in the Christian Middle Ages. There was a renewed interest in Plato in the early Renaissance; Leonardo Bruni, Cardinal Bessarion and a few others translated some of his works into Latin, but widespread access to Platonic texts was limited before the second half of the fifteenth century. The man chiefly responsible for packaging and presenting Plato to Renaissance Italy was Marsiglio Ficino. In 1462 Cosimo de' Medici gave him a manuscript with all 36 of Plato's dialogues in Greek and provided him with a house near the Medici villa at Careggi. Between 1462 and 1469 Ficino translated the works of Plato into Latin, making them accessible to all scholars not just to the minority who could read Greek. He spent the next five years exploring the connections and parallels between Neoplatonism and Christianity and writing his *Theologica Platonica*, a book which discussed the relationship between Christian theology and Plato's ideas on the immortality of the soul. Later, between 1484 and 1492, he translated the works of Plotinus, making available for the first time to the Christian world the thoughts of the founder of classical Neoplatonism. Ficino did more than just study and write. He also taught, not officially at the University of Florence, but informally - rather as Plato had in fifth century Athens at the Academy.

Apart from Ficino, perhaps the best known Neoplatonist was the young and outrageous Pico della Mirandola (1463-94). Pico was a precocious genius who excelled not only in Latin and Greek, but also Hebrew and Arabic. At the age of 23 he published 900 theses, or statements, which he offered to defend against all-comers - a debate banned by the pope because some of his ideas were seen as heretical. Ficino, however, managed to stay on the right side of the Church.

b) Myths about Neoplatonism

The number of Renaissance Neoplatonists has been exaggerated and in recent years scholars have questioned some misleading assertions about the movement - myths which arose from the Neoplatonists' own claims about themselves. It used to be argued that while Aristotle was the most influential philosopher in the Middle Ages, Plato replaced him as such in the Renaissance. In fact Aristotle was not displaced from his central position; he was not neglected by Renaissance thinkers and remained at the heart of most university courses of education, even at Florence. But more important than this was the way the difference between Plato and Aristotle was represented.

When the painter Raphael was decorating a room in the Vatican palace for Pope Julius II, he made Aristotle and Plato the central figures in *The School of Athens* (see the illustration on page 115). He drew a dramatic contrast between them by showing Aristotle with an outstretched hand emphasising the material earth beneath and Plato with a finger pointing up to a spiritual heaven. Whilst this is an over-simplification of the real views of the two Greek philosophers, it represents very well how the Florentine Neoplatonists viewed them. They believed that Aristotle stressed the wholly material nature of mankind, exploring the physical sciences and arguing that there was no soul or spirit which survived the death of the body, whilst Plato foreshadowed the Christian doctrine of the soul, believing that mankind was made up of soul and body, and that the soul survived death.

Aristotle, so the Neoplatonists argued, had been 'Christianised' by St Thomas Aquinas, and when the humanist scholars removed those Christian glosses, they found his materialism conflicted too sharply with their Christian faith; Plato's ideas, on the other hand, allowed all sorts of creative parallels with Christianity to be drawn. In fact, however, both Plato and Aristotle were pagan philosophers whose ideas were at odds with Christianity. The real difference was not between what they thought, but how they were studied in the Renaissance. Aristotle was indeed being subjected to critical scholar-ship which revealed his paganism, but Plato was not.

The students of Plato concentrated on those aspects of his thought which were closest to Christianity, and they neglected and even misrepresented those which were clearly heathen. Translations of Plato from Greek to Latin were not literal, but broadly interpreted the 'sense' of Plato for the modern - i.e. Christian - world, and so glossed over many problems. Neoplatonism was not predominant in Renaissance Italy and there were a number of active anti-Platonists who drew attention to the profoundly unchristian elements of Neoplatonic thinking: the belief that the soul existed before birth; belief in the transmigration of souls (the idea that the soul of a human being could be reincarnated as an animal or bird); and Plato's sympathetic depiction of homosexual love. As a number of anti-Platonist scholars made clear, the Neoplatonists selected carefully from Plato's works and interpreted him in ways which suited their purposes.

A myth has also grown up about Ficino's 'Platonic Academy'. At the villa at Careggi, it was suggested, a community of scholars lived together and students, including the young Michelangelo, flocked from Florence to sit at their feet and listen to Neoplatonic ideas being expounded. Lorenzo the Magnificent, it was claimed, presided over the academy as a benign patron after Cosimo's death. There are, however, a number of problems about this charming picture. Certainly there was a small school, but 'the number of young men fully initiated into the Platonic mysteries was probably quite small'.[7] There is no evidence that Pico, or other leading scholars like Poliziano, the tutor of Lorenzo de' Medici's children, were ever part of a Careggi school. Indeed, the Medici link itself has been exaggerated. Cosimo was a patron of Ficino for only the last two years of his life, and after his death Ficino had sought and found other patrons than Lorenzo. Although his translation of Plato was complete by 1469, it was not published until 1484 and even then the cost was underwritten not by the Medici but the Valori family. Lorenzo played some part in the group's proceedings, but was clearly not the 'presiding patron'. Ficino did teach many of the influential men of Florence informally, but not at Careggi, rather at various places in the city, particularly the church of S. Maria degli Angeli.

c) Neoplatonic Ideas

However, when all the myths about the Neoplatonists have been exposed and all the limitations on them imposed, the fact remains that this small group had a great influence on a number of major Renaissance writers and artists. Their ideas were highly complex, and often a little vague and mystical, so that it is difficult to summarise them without oversimplification. First, there was the idea that human beings had a dual nature which combined body and soul, material and spiritual. Ficino suggested that humankind was on a ladder. At the bottom of the ladder were the animals, who had only one nature - a wholly material one. At the top of the ladder were the angels who also had a single nature, a wholly spiritual one. Mankind combined the two natures, material and spiritual. Neither the animals nor the angels could change their natures but, to an extent, man could. He might develop his spiritual side and so climb up the ladder to be closer to the angels, or he might neglect it and slip down into coarse, bestial behaviour. But only to an extent - humankind would always have a dual nature with some element of the spiritual and of the material in it. Pico suggested that when God created man, he said to Adam:

1   I have set you at the centre of the world, so that from there you may
     more easily survey whatever is in the world. We have made you neither
     heavenly nor earthly, neither mortal nor immortal, so that you may
     fashion yourself in whatever form you shall prefer. You shall be able to
5   descend among the lower forms of being, which are brute beasts; you
     shall be able to be reborn out of the judgement of your own soul into
     the higher beings, which are divine.[8]

This became related to the broader Renaissance view that human beings had two sides to their nature, one active and one contemplative. The perfect human being was one who kept these two sides in balance, who was involved in the world of action and in the world of thought.

Secondly, there was the idea of Platonic love. This argued that there were three kinds of love - sensual, spiritual and divine - each of which led to another in a never-ending circle. Sensual love arose when one was attracted by physical beauty, the face and body of a desired person (the homosexual nature of that love in Plato was deliberately concealed). As one came to know the person better, so sensual love led one into spiritual love, love of the soul not the body, a love which survived and grew after physical beauty had faded. Spiritual love of the soul of a beloved individual led one to divine love - the love of God who created all. So the contemplation of physical beauty could lead one ultimately to God. But this was not only a process of rising from a lower form of love (sensual) to higher forms. In another sense, Platonic love was a circle not a ladder, because divine love of God led you to love the beauty of God's creation and God's greatest creation was humankind. Thus divine love led you back to sensual love of the human body. Hence the concept of Platonic love was much richer and fuller than the limited way the phrase is often used today simply to mean a non-sexual friendship. The way Botticelli may have used these ideas in a painting is discussed on page 113 - indeed, it was largely because these ideas influenced a small group of important Florentine artists that the extent of Neoplatonism in Renaissance Italy has been so much exaggerated.

4 Humanism, Propaganda and History Writing: A Case Study

The traditions of the ancient civilisations of Greece and Rome influenced the way Renaissance Italy developed in a number of areas: in poetry and drama; in science and medicine; in philosophy and in the visual arts. In this section we shall consider, as a case study, the development of the art of writing history. The general points which this example will illustrate also applied in a number of other fields of intellectual activity. Classical models for Renaissance historians were provided by the Greeks, Herodotus and Thucydides, and the Romans, Livy and Tacitus. The histories they wrote told of the brave deeds of great men and were exclusively concerned with political, military and diplomatic matters. But they did seek to explain and interpret as well as to tell a story. In the Middle Ages the art of writing history declined and instead of historians there were chroniclers who listed events. Although they preserved some of the raw material of history, they seldom shaped a narrative or constructed an explanation. It was the humanist historians of Renaissance Italy who recovered the ancient art of history writing and re-founded the historical tradition.

a) Historians of Florence

The humanist chancellor of Florence, Coluccio Salutati, saw a political purpose in history writing, observing that a knowledge of the past inspired princes and taught all men how to act in the present. It was

Salutati's pupil and successor as chancellor, Leonardo Bruni (1370-1444), who wrote a *History of the Florentine People* in 12 books. He based this, in part on Thucydides's Greek *History of the Peloponnesian War*, but chiefly on Livy's Latin *History of Rome*. Livy had begun his history with the foundation of the city, so Bruni did the same, tracing the rise of Florence from a minor Roman colony to a great power. He ended his history in 1402, when the sudden death of Giangaleazzo Visconti saved the city from Milanese domination. Bruni combined the patriotism of the chroniclers with the concept of virtuous, active citizens he found in his classical models. Like these models, his was a political, military and diplomatic history which completely ignored social groupings such as the guilds or the family. This set a pattern of history writing which lasted until the middle of the twentieth century. Later humanists continued the project of writing the History of Florence, first Poggio Bracciolini and then Niccolò Machiavelli.

b) Patronage, Princes and Propaganda

If Bruni was one of the first great humanist historians, Flavio Biondo (1392-1463) was the other. He grew up in Florence and then worked in the papal chancellery in Rome where he wrote a history of Europe from the end of the Roman Empire to his own century. But it was when he entered the service of the King of Naples in 1448 that he did his greatest work. His biography of King Alfonso tells the story of the civil war for the crown of Naples from the perspective of the victor (see page 42). His royal patron was not just subsidising scholarship, he was also purchasing propaganda. History was being written with a 'spin' which flattered his employer. It was because of his willingness to do this that Biondo got the job. His rival for the position had been the humanist and philologist Lorenzo Valla, whose reluctance to massage the ego of his patron led to his being passed over in favour of Biondo.

The Sforza dukes of Milan were quick to see the advantage of a sympathetic historian. Giovanni Simonetta (1410-92) entered the service of Francesco Sforza in 1450 and spent the next 20 years writing a biography of the Duke. He constructed his history from sound sources: his own observations, his interviews with surviving witnesses, documents from the archives of the dukes and the bishops of Milan. He explained events entirely in human terms - divine providence was never invoked. But for all this, his work had a political purpose and was history as propaganda. It is easy, and right, for us to be critical of this. But we should pause before we dismiss it out-of-hand. At least history was being written: men were being employed to shape and explain the events of the past, a tradition and methodology were being established. For the moment, these were being used to serve a political purpose, but those skills could, in time, be employed more impartially. Moreover, what is the real difference between a Biondo or a Simonetta writing history to justify and praise princes who paid them, and civic patriots like Bruni justifying and praising the city of which they were a part?

c) Francesco Guicciardini 1483-1540

The greatest of the humanist historians, Francesco Guicciardini, who took history writing to a new level, was also a patriotic Florentine. His was one of the political families of the Republic and he was proud of the part his ancestors had played in the history of their city. Guicciardini saw himself principally as a politician, a diplomat and an administrator who wrote history only in his spare time. He came of age politically when Giovanni de' Medici became Pope and the fate of Florence was tied to that of Rome. Although he was critical of the Church, he spent most of his life in the employment of the two Medici Popes, Leo X and Clement VII. But he worked for them in an administrative and diplomatic role; when he wrote history he wrote it independently, for himself. In the three years after the Sack of Rome of 1527, when his papal employer was exiled from Rome, he set out to write the history of Florence and in doing so, began to develop a new methodology. Hitherto, humanist historians had structured their work largely around a single source. Additional information would be subservient to the shape provided by the main account and history was seen, essentially, as a branch of literature. History, it was agreed, should contain 'nothing false', but that was interpreted as meaning nothing that was morally false. A precise chronology and painstaking factual accuracy was less important than the literary flow of the narrative and its ultimate moral purpose. Guicciardini, however, based his work on detailed archival research not only on his own family papers, but also on the archives of the other great families in the city and of the commune itself. The complexity of such an undertaking was unprecedented, and Guicciardini left this work unfinished.

Three years later when the second Medici Pope was dead and Guicciardini was unemployed again, he decided to write instead a history of Italy from 1494 to the present day. The *Storia d'Italia* (1537-40), the greatest achievement of his life, is considered by many to be the first modern work of history. He recognised that it was impossible to tell the story of Florence in this period without examining also events in the other Italian states, so he constructed a skilful narrative which moved easily from place to place as the unfolding events required. After a few pages explaining events in Milan, he moved to Rome, Florence, Venice and back to Milan in an easy way which was quite unprecedented. Moreover, although his history is a narrative, it is an *explanatory* narrative: it tells the story in such a way that it provides an explanation of events, it explores cause and effect and answers the analytical questions which historians need to ask. In the last three years of his life, Francesco Guicciardini produced not only a literary masterpiece, but also a masterly work of historical interpretation.

This discussion of the development of the art of history writing in Renaissance Italy has been offered as a case study. It is an example of one of the many fields in which Renaissance thinking was influenced by the ancient civilisations of Greece and Rome. Just as in other areas, Renaissance historians were not only inspired by the tradition of the Ancient World but also influenced by the practical demands of the present. They produced something distinctive: their work was affected by the classical models, but was not identical to them. Contemporary politics and the interests of their patrons also influenced what they wrote.

5 Conclusion

The arts syllabus of Renaissance schools and universities - the *studia humanitatis* - consisted of the study of Latin (and, for a few students, Greek) texts dealing with grammar, rhetoric, history, poetry, moral philosophy and civic patriotism. At its heart, the Italian Renaissance was about Christian humanist scholars reading Latin and Greek texts. They searched out documents and restored them, as best they could, to their ancient purity. All scholars read Latin, and a few read Greek, but translations of Greek works into Latin, like Ficino's translations of Plato, made their ideas widely available. What they read, they copied and soon Italian historians were writing the history of their own times in the style of the ancient writers. A new enthusiasm for the Ancient World grew: antique sculptures and ruins of ancient buildings were uncovered, classical coins and medals were collected, Latin manuals on warfare were studied and recommended to contemporary soldiers. But at its heart, the Renaissance's revival of antiquity was about books and the study of the classical languages and texts. As John Hale properly warns us: 'unless the word 'humanism' retains the smell of the scholar's lamp it will mislead'.[9]

References

1   H. Baron, *The Crisis of the Early Italian Renaissance* (Princeton University Press, 1955), p. 38.
2   *The Oxford English Dictionary* Vol. VIII, (OUP, 1933).
3   *Portable Renaissance Reader*, pp. 132-3.
4   James Hankins, *Plato in the Italian Renaissance* Vol. One (Brill, 1990), p. 29.
5   Chambers and Pullan, *Venice*, pp. 357-8.
6   Martin Lowry, *The World of Aldus Manutius: Business and Scholarship in Renaissance Venice* (Blackwell, 1979), p. 304.
7   Hankins, *Plato*, p. 298.
8   Pico della Mirandola, *Oration on the Dignity of Man* 1469-74, reprinted in *Portable Renaissance Reader*, p. 478.
9   Hale, *Encyclopaedia*, p. 171.

Summary Diagram
The Ancient World and Renaissance Humanism

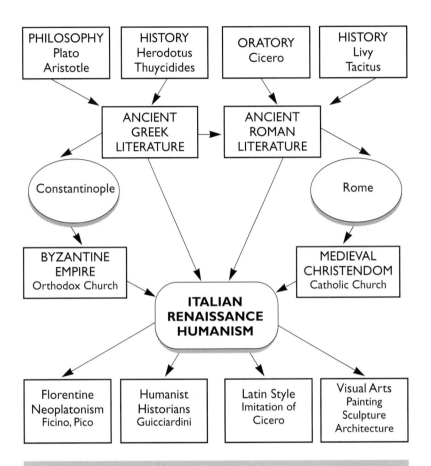

1. Latin, Greek and Books
Read the extracts from Valla, Bruni and Bessarion, pages 70, 72 and 73, then answer the following questions.
a) Why does Valla rate the Latin language more highly than the political power of the Roman Empire? (3 marks)
b) What do these three extracts tell you about the values of humanist scholars? What were the things they valued most, and why? (4 marks)
c) What do these three extracts tell us about the role of language and books in the transmission of ideas down the centuries? (3 marks)

Answering essay questions on 'The Ancient World and Renaissance Humanism'

1. What did humanist scholars do and why were their activities significant?
2. Account for the development of Greek studies in Italy in general and of Neoplatonism in particular, and discuss how they affected the thinking of Italian Renaissance scholars and artists.
3. Why and how did the art of history writing develop in Renaissance Italy?

The Use of Quotations in Essays

There are two main sorts of quotations you can use in essays. One is quotation from the primary sources (i.e. those written during the period being studied); the other is from the secondary sources (i.e. those from present day historians). Quotations from primary sources can be valuable, but should be used with restraint. A short quotation, perhaps just a brief phrase, is sometimes better than a longer one of a whole sentence. Do not be misled by what authors do in books. As we observed earlier, books are very different from essays. Often in a book, the author wants to give a flavour of a writer's style, so may quote a lengthy passage of several lines. But an essay needs to be more directed and controlled than this. Only quote something which makes a specific point directly relevant to the question. Use the quotation, discuss it; do not just put it in for decoration. It must be a vital part of the argument, not an ornament. A short phrase is much more likely to be direct and specific than a longer passage - remember you need a scalpel, not a blunt instrument. Used well, a quotation from the primary sources is a valuable piece of evidence and can show you operating as an historian in an excellent way.

Quotation from the secondary sources is much more of a problem. Most students quote too much; it is almost always better to put things in your own words. There are always one or two exceptions, but generally speaking you should quote from the secondary sources only in the following cases:

a) When you disagree with the writer. You might, for example, take a phrase from Burckhardt and then demolish what he says.

b) When you can quote two modern historians who disagree with each other. Brief quotation is often a good way of introducing a modern historiographical controversy.

c) When the author is the outstanding specialist authority and has put forward a new theory or interpretation which you do not find elsewhere. Michael Mallett on the Borgias or James Hankin on the Neoplatonists may come into this category, but, as in the case of the primary sources, make sure it is a brief, specific quotation which you discuss and use in your argument.

Always think twice before quoting a textbook which merely summarises other peoples' arguments, or which makes ordinary points repeated by a wide range of writers. You will only develop your own style by writing in your own words and you should do this as much as you can.

In short, do not quote too much and 'if in doubt, leave it out'.

7 Renaissance Man and the Real World

Writers and thinkers in the fifteenth century had an ideal of what a human being should be; the reality of what Renaissance people were actually like, of course, was rather different. This chapter explores the distance between the ideal and the reality. In the last chapter we considered the scholars of Renaissance Italy in terms of their direct connections with the Ancient World. In this chapter we concentrate on the new and the impact on Renaissance thinking of current events like the French invasion of 1494. In particular we examine how far the ideal of a perfect 'Renaissance Man', who was both soldier and scholar, was removed from the reality of the mercenary soldiers of the age. Finally we discuss how this conflict between the ideal and the real was explored in the works of Machiavelli.

1 Soldier and Scholar: A Renaissance Ideal

One of the best known Renaissance images is a drawing by Leonardo, illustrated on page 85, of a naked man with arms and legs outstretched standing inside a circle and a square. This is called Vitruvian Man, after the ancient Roman architect, Vitruvius, who explained human proportion in this way. Buildings, almost always symmetrical in design, could be given a human scale by adopting corresponding proportions for their height and width. The Greek Pythagoras, some of whose ideas were incorporated into Neoplatonism, discovered that all the intervals in a musical scale could be expressed as ratios of whole numbers. On this simple, numerical basis elaborate harmonies could be developed. Pythagoras believed harmony had cosmic significance; as the earth, sun, moon and five known planets (he called them the spheres) whirled through space at different speeds they produced different sounds which made up the eight notes of a scale - this was the harmony of the spheres. This balanced and harmonious view of the cosmos was still widely held throughout the Renaissance until the Scientific Revolution of the seventeenth century.

The symmetry and proportion of a Renaissance building, or the harmony of a piece of music, made up an objective standard of beauty. The idea that 'beauty lies in the eye of the beholder' was not one Renaissance people shared; to them beauty was harmony, symmetry, proportion and number. These standards were applied not just to architecture and music but also to human beings. From Burckhardt's *Civilization of the Renaissance in Italy* (1860) onwards, much has been made of the idea of a Universal Man - *l'uomo universale*. Universality was, in fact, less important in the concept of Renaissance Man than harmony. The ideal person was one who had a balanced personality, and the crucial balance was that between the active and

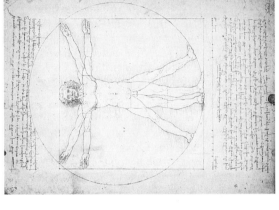

Leonardo da Vinci: Vitruvian Man (Venice, Accademia). This drawing relates the proportions of the human body to the geometrically perfect shapes of the circle and the square. The span of a man's arms held at right angles to his body should be the same as his height and so he fits perfectly in the square; a man, with legs apart and arms raised, will touch with his hands and feet the circumference of a circle of which his navel is the centre. Leonardo has written the text above and below the drawing backwards so that it has to be held to a mirror to be read

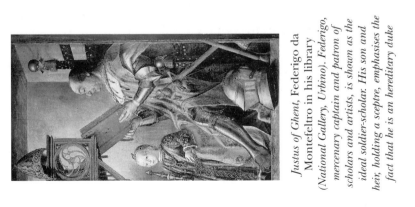

Justus of Ghent, Federigo da Montefeltro in his library (National Gallery, Urbino). Federigo, mercenary captain and patron of scholars and artists, is shown as the ideal soldier-scholar. His son and heir, holding a sceptre, emphasises the fact that he is an hereditary duke

contemplative, between arms and letters, between the soldier and the scholar.

The man who best exemplified this ideal was Federigo da Montefeltro, Duke of Urbino (1422-82) - an outstanding military leader and a patron of artists and scholars. In his palace at Urbino, a remote hill town in the Apennines, he built up a great library of manuscripts and employed artists like the young Raphael. He was a mercenary captain, then a highly respectable profession, who was employed, in turn, by the papacy, Venice and Florence. The Florentine bookseller, Vespasiano, wrote an account of his life, first describing the duke's military achievements, then considering

> 1 in what high esteem the Duke held all Greek and Latin writers, sacred as well as secular. He alone had a mind to do what no one had done for a thousand years or more; that is, to create the finest library since ancient times. He spared neither cost nor labour, and when he knew of
> 5 a fine book, whether in Italy or not, he would send for it. It is now 14 or more years since he began the library, and he always employed, in Urbino, in Florence and in other places, 30 or 40 scribes in his service.[1]

Such literary efforts were close to the bookseller's heart, but he knew it was the combination of these scholarly pursuits with his formidable reputation as a soldier that made Federigo special. The Duke epitomised the Renaissance idea of balance by

> 1 his knowledge of the Latin tongue, taken in connection with military affairs, for it is difficult for a leader to excel in arms unless he be, like the Duke, a man of letters, seeing that the past is a mirror of the present. A military leader who knows Latin has a great advantage over one who
> 5 does not.[2]

The portrait by Justus of Ghent painted in the 1470s and illustrated on page 85, shows Federigo in his library reading a manuscript, dressed in armour with his helmet by his side - the perfect example of the man of thought and of action, the soldier and the scholar. In *The Book of the Courtier*, Castiglione sought to describe the perfect courtier. His book takes the form of a discussion in the court at Urbino in 1507 when Federigo's son - the young boy in Justus de Ghent's portrait - was Duke. The ideal courtier he described was a many talented man who combined the qualities of a soldier and a scholar. But, in reality, there were few such men about. Federigo da Montefeltro is always cited as the example because there were so few others who fitted the bill. He was not typical but exceptional. Renaissance Man as soldier and scholar was an ideal which existed chiefly in the minds of writers and thinkers. One event more than any other revealed the fictional nature of this ideal - the French invasion of Italy in 1494.

2 The French Invasion of 1494

This book is not concerned with the details of military and diplomatic history, but the events of 1494 had so traumatic an effect upon the minds of Renaissance Italians that we must examine them. Historians today do not consider this French invasion as important in political terms as those alive at the time thought it was; our concern here is not with its practical political impact, but with the effect it had upon the minds of Renaissance Italians and the way it made them perceive the world and themselves. Castiglione claimed that the combination in one person of the soldier and the scholar, of arms and letters, was a characteristically Italian virtue not shared or valued by the French who:

> ı recognize only the nobility of arms and think nothing of all the rest; and
> so they not only do not appreciate learning but detest it, regarding men
> of letters as basely inferior and thinking it a great insult to call anyone a
> scholar ... I blame the French for believing that letters are harmful to
> 5 the profession of arms, and I maintain myself that it is more fitting for a
> warrior to be educated than for anyone else; and I would have these
> two accomplishments, the one helping the other, as is most fitting, joined
> together in one courtier.³

Yet, in 1494, a decade before Castiglione was writing, the French had invaded Italy and conquered Naples meeting no real resistance. According to the ideal, Italian soldier-scholars should easily have defeated them, but in reality the Italians had shown 'a lack of valour on the battlefield'.

Therefore in the following narrative we shall examine not only what happened, but also how contemporaries viewed events, mainly through the eyes of Francesco Guicciardini in his *History of Italy*. In Chapter four we examined the political history of the major Italian states up to the eve of the French invasion in 1494; this narrative takes up where that chapter left off. In Italy in 1494, contemporaries believed, a golden age of stability was ending. Guicciardini reflected:

> ı Italy had never known such prosperity or such a desirable condition as
> that which it enjoyed in all tranquillity in the year 1490 and the years
> immediately before and after. For all at peace and quietness, knowing no
> other rule than that of its own people, Italy was not only rich in popu-
> 5 lation, merchandise and wealth, but she was adorned to the highest
> degree by the magnificence of many princes, by the splendour of innu-
> merable noble and beautiful cities, by the throne and majesty of religion;
> full of men most able in the administration of public affairs, and of noble
> minds learned in every branch of study and versed in every worthy art
> and skill.⁴

Modern historians tell us this was a false picture, that the 40 years before the French invasion were not as peaceful, as stable or as idyllic as Guicciardini suggested, but the important point is that contemporaries *believed* they were. As they looked around the peninsula they saw that stability coming to an end. In 1492 the Pope died and the worldly Rodrigo Borgia was elected Pope Alexander VI. In the same year, in Florence, Lorenzo de' Medici died and was succeeded by his inexperienced son, Piero. In 1494 Ferrante, who had sat on the throne of Naples for nearly 36 years, died and his unpopular son Alfonso became king. In Milan in 1494 the sickly Giovan Galeazzo Sforza died and his young son was passed over in the succession, the dukedom going to his uncle, Lodovico il Moro.

A few months earlier, Lodovico il Moro's ambition had led him to invite Charles VIII of France to invade Italy. In 1494 Charles was 24 years old. He had become King of France in 1483 at the age of 13. Although he was mocked by contemporaries for his physical appearance - he was extremely short with a skinny body topped by a large head and massive nose - he was a man of ambition and romantic vision. He dreamed of becoming King of Naples (the French had quite a good claim) and then using the kingdom as a base from which to launch a crusade to recapture Constantinople from the Turks. When Lodovico Sforza invited him to invade Italy to pursue the French claim to the throne of Naples, he was playing politics. Many Italian princes before him had invited in foreigners who had never come, but the threat had strengthened their diplomatic hand. But Charles VIII did come, and the Sforzas of Milan were amongst the first to regret it.

Because of the Milanese invitation, the Alpine passes were open for the French army to march freely into Italy. Once there, they met no real resistance. In the east, Venice refused to take sides. The French marched south through Milan into Tuscany. Piero de' Medici, concerned about the volume of Florentine trade in France and lacking his father's diplomatic skills, was no match for the charm and skill of the French dwarf. He promised 200,000 ducats as a loan to fund the French war effort and Charles VIII entered the city of Florence as a conqueror. Pisa, which had been under Florentine control for 90 years was given its liberty by the French. Piero fell from power in Florence, bringing to an end 60 years of Medici domination. Charles continued south, still encountering no resistance. He entered Rome and met the Borgia Pope in the gardens of the Vatican. Alexander VI had no choice but to promise him the crown of Naples and to encourage him to crusade against the Turks. After the worst of the winter had passed, Charles VIII entered Naples on 24 February 1495.

On 20 May 1495, soon after his formal coronation as King of Naples, Charles VIII left the city for ever and returned to France. (He was to die three years later after hitting his large head on a low doorway in his palace.) In Naples, his lines of communication with France were too extended and difficult to maintain. Pope Alexander VI had built an alliance of states against him; the Florentine republic, then under the sway of Savonarola, was the only major state still to support the French. The Kingdom of Naples was difficult to govern at the best of times and Charles had no taste for a long civil war of succession. The immediate consequence of the invasion was slight, but it set a precedent and other foreign invasions followed in the next 30 odd years, culminating in the Sack of Rome by the Spanish Imperial forces of the Emperor Charles V in 1527.

The most important effect of Charles VIII's invasion was on the Italian psyche. Guicciardini described 1494 as 'a most unhappy year for Italy, and truly the beginning of years of wretchedness'.[5] The Italian failure to withstand the French invasion blighted a whole generation. Guicciardini, Machiavelli and dozens of others, struggled to come to terms with the shame and to explain the disaster. This was a problem which not even the distinctly soft-centred Castiglione (notorious for sitting on fences and burying his head in the sand) could evade, though he sought to avoid the painful memory:

> it would be more shameful for us to make this known to the world than it is for the French to be ignorant of letters, so it is better to pass over in silence what we cannot recall without sorrow.[6]

The model of the soldier-scholar as the consummate man was punctured by the reality of the Italian defeat at the hands of the French. If the ideal of a balanced Renaissance Man who combined arms and letters was to survive, then that defeat had to be explained; the most common humanist line was to blame the mercenaries.

3 Mercenaries and their Critics

Federigo da Montefeltro, the great exemplar of the ideal Renaissance Man, had been a mercenary captain. If that ideal were to survive the defeat by the French, it was important to establish that the mercenaries employed by the Italian states in 1494 were not soldier-scholars. This was not difficult for the humanists to do. Although they admired Federigo, in general they disliked mercenaries. The tradition of civic humanism led them to praise citizen militias and denigrate the employment of mercenaries (see page 71). They believed that men fighting for the city they loved would be more effective than those fighting for money. But once again, in seeking to preserve the ideal, the humanist scholars were out of touch with reality. The fault for the Italian defeat in 1494 lay less with the effectiveness of the mercenary armies than with the lack of political will of the princes who employed them. In this section we shall examine what mercenary armies were really like, so that we can see more clearly how far removed from contemporary reality the ideals of the humanists were.

It was in the twentieth century that mercenary soldiering became seen as a dirty job. In Renaissance Italy it was a highly respectable occupation. Apart from a handful of humanist scholars, contemporaries respected them. Florence was an exception in distrusting her mercenaries, treating them badly and thus being ill-served by them. Most other cities had a good relationship with their *condottieri* or mercenary captains, none better than Venice which rewarded them not only with money, but also with palaces, statues and occasionally even entry to the Great Council - an extremely rare honour.

a) Mercenary Armies

A Renaissance army was made up of many different elements. At its heart would usually be a state's permanent company, such as the prince's bodyguard, the family troops, or the city guard. To this would be added several mercenary companies. These would include specialist infantry and artillery forces, as well as basic cavalry units. Each company was led by a *condottiero*, and one of these would be appointed captain-general to command the entire army. Beneath the captain-general was a council of senior *condottieri* some of whom were distinguished by the rank of marshal. Each *condottiero* signed a contract (a *condotte*) with the state who employed him. This would specify the number of troops he would provide, how long the contract would last, how much he would be paid and how the contract should be concluded. For cavalry, the size of the company was normally expressed as a number of lances. A lance was a small group of men, necessary to maintain in the field an armoured knight, on horseback. Until 1450 most lances consisted of three men; later the development of heavy cavalry with weightier armour made four or five men common. The length of the contract was usually agreed in two parts. First there would be a fixed term of service, then an optional extension period for which the contract could be renewed. In the early fifteenth century, both of these were normally six months and it was unusual for a *condottiero* to fight for a state for more than a year at a time. Later, a fixed period of two years, with an extension for another year became common. Venice led the trend for longer contracts, Florence resisted it, but the more mercenaries were trusted, the better they served their masters.

Italian armies changed over the period of the Renaissance. Mercenary companies were trusted more and treated better by their employers. Their critics claimed they became old-fashioned, failing to keep up with military developments in the rest of Europe, but this is not entirely fair. Cavalry was becoming heavier and armour was reaching a weight where knights were unable to move when they fell off their horses. Increasingly, they were supplemented by light cavalry with mounted crossbow men and mounted handgun men. The Venetians introduced to Italy *stradiots* from Albania - lancers on light, unarmoured horses, with great manoeuvrability. Amongst the foot-soldiers, the large untrained forces of the thirteenth century were replaced by small, highly trained infantry companies. Until about

1450 these consisted of three equal parts, infantry lances, shield-bearers and crossbow men. These combined to provide a fairly static wall to withstand cavalry advance. In the second half of the fifteenth century there were two main developments in infantry fighting: first the use of lightly armed men with sword and buckler who were agile and could engage in hand-to-hand combat; secondly the development of hand firearms. In all these developments, Italian armies may have been a little behind the times, but only a little. Moreover, it was highly-trained, specialist companies of mercenaries that brought them up-to-date with modern developments, not untrained militia.

b) Humanist Criticisms of the Mercenaries

Of course there were exceptions, but on the whole mercenaries fighting for the Italian states were trained professionals. Most were not soldier-scholars; most did not exhibit the ideal qualities of the balanced Renaissance man. It is true that a few well-educated *condottieri* read classical treatises on war for their own entertainment, but they did not read them to learn how to fight in the real world of Renaissance Italy. Humanists naively thought they should. They believed that the example of the Ancient World should dictate the military tactics of contemporary armies. These desk-bound theorists studied the Roman histories of Caesar and Livy, adopted the military values of the Ancient World, and criticised the mercenaries for not sharing them. The chief value was fighting for one's country not money - so, Guicciardini grumbled:

1   the men-at-arms were either peasants or plebians subject to some other prince and completely dependent on the captains with whom they contracted for their salaries. The captains were very rarely subjects of those whom they served; besides they often had different interests
5   and ends. Unstable, they frequently passed from one service to another, sometimes tempted by ambition or greed or other interests to be not only unstable but faithless.[7]

Machiavelli moaned that:

1   Mercenaries are disunited, thirsty for power, undisciplined and disloyal; they are brave among their friends and cowards before the enemy; they avoid defeat just so long as they avoid battle; in peacetime you are despoiled by them, and in wartime by the enemy. The reason for all this
5   is that there is no loyalty or inducement to keep them on the field apart from the little they are paid, and this is not enough to make them want to die for you... The present ruin of Italy has been caused by nothing else but the reliance placed on mercenary troops for so many years.[8]

Even the courtier Castiglione suggested that the disaster of 1494 could be blamed on the mercenaries:

the weakness of a few has inflicted grave misfortune along with lasting infamy on the many, and they are responsible for our ruin and the way our spirit has been weakened if not crushed.[9]

Like Guicciardini, Machiavelli was a Florentine, 'whose experience of the *condottieri* was largely limited to the one army in Italy which had failed to achieve the permanence and professionalism of those of the other major states.'[10] In 1505 he was given the opportunity to establish and train a Florentine citizen militia; he did so with characteristic enthusiasm and energy. But those conscripted to it resented the fact and, although it played a small part in the siege of Pisa, it failed to distinguish itself. In theory citizens fighting for their own country might be more admirable, but in practice trained mercenaries were more effective in the art of war.

We have argued so far in this chapter that the humanists' ideal of what Renaissance man should be was at odds with the realities of contemporary life, particularly as far as military matters were concerned. Yet one humanist, Machiavelli, claimed, in *The Prince*,

1   I have thought it proper to represent things as they are in real truth, rather than as they are imagined. Many have dreamed up republics which have never in truth been known to exist; the gulf between how one should live and how one does live is so wide that a man who neglects
5   what is actually done for what should be done learns the way to self-destruction rather than self-preservation.[11]

He has been widely regarded as the greatest advocate of *Realpolitik* - politics determined by practical, rather than moral or ideological, considerations. In the last section of this chapter we shall consider the life and ideals of Machiavelli and ask just how far he was a realist.

4 Machiavelli, Political Morality and the New Prince

Machiavelli's *The Prince* is an easy book to read but a difficult one to understand.[12] It had the reputation of being a notorious, wicked, immoral book, but if you read it without understanding the context in which it was written you may wonder what all the fuss was about. When you have mastered that context, it is thrilling, daring, breathtaking, a book which challenged a thousand-year tradition of Christian political thought. To understand *The Prince* you need first to know something about Machiavelli's life, then about the political theory of medieval and Renaissance Christendom which preceded it.

a) Machiavelli's Life

Niccolò Machiavelli was born in Florence in 1469, the year in which the 20-year-old Lorenzo the Magnificent became the dominant personality in the city. He was 25 when the French invaded and the Medici fell, 29 when Savonarola, of whom he disapproved, was burned. We know nothing of his life in this period. For 14 years after the death of Savonarola, Florence functioned as a genuine Republic, with no single dominant family. The constitution was adapted to make it a little more like the Venetian and in 1502 Piero Soderini was elected as *Gonfalonier* for Life, similar to the Doge of Venice - no 'prince of Florence' but a servant of the Republic. From 1498 to 1512, Machiavelli served this republic as bureaucrat, diplomat and administrator. Throughout his public career, he was always in second-rank posts. The Chancellor of Florence was an important position to which eminent humanists like Salutati and Bruni were appointed; Machiavelli was Second Chancellor, one of a number of assistants who carried out the routine business. He witnessed and recorded important decisions of state, but those decisions were made by the elected citizens. He went on a number of diplomatic missions to various Italian princes, to the King of France, to the Holy Roman Emperor and to the pope, but always as second-in-command; others made the important decisions. He met Cesare Borgia twice at the height of his power and was so much impressed by him that when he met him again at the time of his fall he was still too dazzled to notice his faults (see page 60). But generally his judgement was sound and his analysis acute, even in his very first report - on the factions in Pistoia, a subject city of Florence.

His jobs may have been always second-rank, but for a decade and a half Machiavelli was at the heart of Florentine politics, observing at first-hand the political events and decisions of the day. He loved it. His passion for politics was overwhelming, all consuming. Later, out of office, he wrote

> Fortune has decreed that as I don't know how to discuss the silk trade or the wool business, or profits and losses, I am left with politics to talk about, and unless I take a vow of silence I must discuss them.[13]

Losing office was, for him, the disaster of his life. In 1512 the Medici were restored to power in Florence by a papal army, Soderini was exiled and Machiavelli, closely associated with him, was arrested, interrogated and tortured. He was exiled to a small village, San Casciano, about two hours walk from Florence, which he was still allowed to visit. But his contact with political life was severed and, for Machiavelli, this was the greatest deprivation. He discussed politics in a couple of correspondences, one with Vettori the Florentine ambassador at the papal court of Leo X, the other with Francesco Guicciardini, currently employed as an administrator by the Medici Pope. But mainly he absorbed himself in a study of the politics of the Ancient World.

Machiavelli was a humanist; as a child he learned Latin and in his exile he read the poets, orators and historians of classical Rome. He wrote satirical poetry, a dialogue on language, and a bawdy play about seduction and impotence which was performed before Pope Leo X. But most of all he read, thought, talked and wrote politics. In a letter to Vettori, dated 10 December 1513 he described the emptiness and frustration of his life in exile: walking around his small farm, drinking and playing cards with peasants in the local inn, killing time. But the night was devoted to his books, to Latin and politics:

1   When evening comes, I return home and go into my study. On the threshold I strip off my muddy, sweaty, workday clothes, and put on the robes of court and palace, and in this graver dress I enter the antique courts of the ancients and am welcomed by them, and there I taste the
5   food that alone is mine, and for which I was born. And there I make bold to speak to them and ask the motives of their actions, and they, in their humanity, reply to me. And for the space of four hours I forget the world, remember no vexation, fear poverty no more, tremble no more at death: I pass indeed into their world... I have written down what I
10 have gained from their conversation, and composed a small work *De principatibus*, where I dive as deep as I can into ideas about this subject, discussing the nature of princely rule.[14]

These were the circumstances in which *The Prince* (1513) was written. In it Machiavelli discussed the state of Italy and the nature of politics and in doing so he used examples from his own experience of recent events and from his classical reading as if they were interchangeable. Some regard *The Discourses* (1513-19), a commentary and series of reflections on Livy's *History of Rome*, as his mature masterpiece, but this lacks the pungency and sting of the briefer, pithier *Prince*.

b) Machiavelli's *The Prince*

In *The Prince* Machiavelli does two main things. Firstly he analyses the present state of Italy and proposes a solution to her problems; secondly he develops a new, secular code of political morality which challenges the age-old tradition of Christian political thought. His analysis of Italy's ills, in the wake of the invasion of 1494 and the foreign wars which followed it, is acute and uncompromising; his proposed solution 'a beautiful, audacious, formidable dream'.[15] He examined the various political institutions in the Italian states and showed how they all lacked vigour, energy and life. He showed the decline of political life in Italy, the lack of civic pride and devotion of people to the state. Then, in a final chapter which bears little relation to the rest of the book, he called for a new prince to come forward 'to liberate Italy from the barbarian' by freeing her from the foreign armies and re-establishing liberty. It was not a realistic or convincing option and in this, as in his hatred of the mercenaries, Machiavelli was as divorced from reality as the other humanist scholars. If this had been all it was, the book would have been soon forgotten.

But in the process of this analysis, *The Prince* develops something startlingly new. It identifies the fundamental paradox in Renaissance thought and culture - the conflict between the classical and the Christian traditions - and it resolves it in a revolutionary way. The value systems, the morality, of the ancient, pagan world had been turned upside down by Christianity and nowhere was this change more problematic than in politics and government. Machiavelli had no quarrel with Christian morality as it applied to private life - there humility and forgiveness, suffering in silence and self-sacrifice, were admirable and made individuals good citizens. But applied to public life, to the activities of governments, he considered such a moral code disastrous. If a foreign invader demanded one province, should one give him two? If violent men flouted the law, should one turn the other cheek? To apply the moral teaching of Christianity to the actions of the prince in the public execution of his duty was to invite disaster.

Machiavelli was not, of course, the first to see the potential conflict between Christian morality and what was politically necessary. Indeed medieval Christian thinkers had evolved an entire theology of 'the just war'. A tradition of Christian 'handbooks for princes' had grown up which advocated that the prince should rule, whenever possible, as a Christian gentleman. But even these accepted that occasionally there might be exceptional circumstances when the prince was required to act outside Christian morality - the traditional maxim was 'necessity has no law'. Machiavelli claimed 'necessity is always with us'. In other words, the occasions when a prince is required, for the good of his state and subjects, to act contrary to Christian principles were not occasional but all the time.

Machiavelli believed in strong government which brought peace, security and prosperity to the people. He believed that Christian morality would lead to weak government, lawlessness and anarchy. Is it better, he asked, to be cruel or compassionate? The Christian would opt for compassion, but in public life, Machiavelli believed, he or she would be wrong to do so. He drew on his own experiences for an example:

1 Cesare Borgia was accounted cruel; nevertheless this cruelty of his reformed the Romagna, brought it unity and restored order and obedience. On reflection, it will be seen that there was more compassion in Cesare than in the Florentine people, who, to escape being called cruel,
5 allowed Pistoia to be devastated. So a prince must not worry if he incurs reproach for his cruelty so long as he keeps his subjects united and loyal. By making an example or two he will prove more compassionate than those who, being too compassionate, allow disorders which lead to murder and rapine. Those nearly always harm the whole community,
10 whereas executions ordered by the prince only affect individuals.[16]

Christian morality forbade the prince to sacrifice individuals for the sake of the community; it never allowed him to use immoral means however good the end might be. Machiavelli argued that the prince could act against individuals in any way necessary, with no moral constraints at all, to achieve an end which was of benefit to the whole community, to the state. He does not say that princes can do anything they like, just anything that is *necessary*. The public good is the only end which justifies the use of any means. In the 24 short chapters of *The Prince*, necessity is invoked 76 times. He was prepared to follow this logic wherever it led, even to statements which, on the surface, appeared outrageous:

> 1 a prudent ruler cannot, and must not honour his word when it places
>   him at a disadvantage and when the reasons for which he made his
>   promise no longer exist. If all men were good, this precept would not
>   be good; but because men are wretched creatures who would not keep
> 5 their word to you, you need not keep your word to them.[17]

In arguing that Christian morality is inapplicable to political life, Machiavelli was challenging the established thought of the day. The reaction was predictable. He was maligned and condemned across Europe. In Elizabethan England, Shakespeare makes one of his most wicked creations boast he will, 'set the murderous Machiavel to school'.[18] Everywhere Machiavelli was denounced as the devil and depicted as a man who urged princes to behave immorally. In a world in which Christianity was seen as the only moral code, such a view was understandable. Even those who admitted that Machiavelli was very accurate in describing how princes actually did behave, thought that it was still wrong of them to do so - a position summed up in the words of the English philosopher Francis Bacon who said Machiavelli wrote 'what men do, and not what they ought to do'.[19]

But seen from today's perspective, his contemporaries were unfair to Machiavelli. Viewed from a pluralist society which accepts that there can be a number of different moral codes all of which are valid, it is possible to say that *The Prince* is anti-Christian but not immoral. There is no doubt that Machiavelli's political morality was different from and hostile to Christianity - but it was neither amoral nor immoral. Rather, Machiavelli claimed, this was how princes *ought* to behave for the well-being of their state and people. What he was advocating for political life was, as he himself recognised, the pagan moral code of the Ancient World. He implied this in *The Prince* and spelled it out clearly in *The Discourses*:

> 1 If one asks oneself how it comes about that people of old were more
>   fond of liberty than they are today, I think the answer is that it is due to
>   the same cause that makes men today less bold than they used to be;
>   and this is due, I think, to the difference between our religion and the
> 5 religion of those days. For our religion leads us to ascribe less esteem
>   to worldly honour... Our religion has glorified humble and contempla-

tive men, rather than men of action. It has assigned as man's greatest good humility, abnegation, and contempt for mundane things, whereas the other identified it with magnanimity, bodily strength, and everything
10 else that conduces to make men very bold. And if our religion demands that in you there be strength, what it asks for is strength to suffer rather than strength to do bold things.[20]

For over a thousand years, since the conversion of Constantine and the adoption of Christianity as the official religion of the Roman Empire, there had been, in theory, a single morality which governed both public and private life. What Machiavelli did was to separate the two; to leave Christianity to control the personal behaviour of private men, but to replace it in public life with a new secular political morality, which echoed the public morality of the classical world and recognised that firm government required a code which allowed the public good to justify harsh treatment of individuals. He was one of the few people to see clearly the fundamental incompatibility of classical and Christian values. In doing so, he struck at the very heart of the Renaissance.

5 Conclusion

Renaissance people studied Greek and Latin writers to learn about the world and themselves. The old adage that medieval man studied God and Renaissance man studied mankind is, as we have seen, too sweeping and in danger of misleading us. But there is still a grain of truth in it. Humanists wanted to understand the nature of humanity; they wanted to know who man was and they evolved a vision of the ideal human being. Humanist scholarship was the activity of a tiny minority of the population, but did its ideal of man have a wider application? As an ideal, it represented what man *could* and *should* be, not what he was. This lack of reality was brought home cruelly by the traumatic events of 1494, when the French conquered Italy armed only with a stick of chalk, as Machiavelli said, to mark the doors of the houses where they would billet their soldiers. This event shattered the humanists' theories, and they, in return, blamed the mercenaries. But the very act of doing so only underlined how out of touch humanist scholars were with the military realities of the day. Machiavelli was as unrealistic as the other humanists in this respect, but in other ways he too shattered long held but untenable theories. The idea that Christian principles could guide the successful ruler of a state was powerfully challenged in *The Prince* and the moral unity of the public and private spheres which, in theory, had dominated a thousand years of Christian government was exposed to the harsh winds of reality. Machiavelli's depiction of mankind as 'ungrateful, fickle, liars, and deceivers...'[21] was a far cry from the ideal Renaissance man of the theorists, but may have been closer to the reality of Renaissance life.

References

1 Vespesiano, *Princes, Popes and Prelates*, p. 102.
2 *Ibid*, p. 99.
3 Castiglione, *The Book of the Courtier* (Penguin Books, 1967), pp. 88, 93.
4 David Abulafia (ed.), *The French Descent into Renaissance Italy, 1494-95: Antecedents and effects* (Variorum, 1995), pp. 18-19.
5 *Ibid*, p. 19.
6 Castiglione, *Courtier*, p. 90.
7 F. Guicciardini, *The History of Italy* (Macmillan, 1969), p. 52.
8 Machiavelli, *Prince*, pp. 77-8.
9 Castiglione, *Courtier*, p. 90.
10 Michael Mallett, *Mercenaries and their Masters: Warfare in Renaissance Italy* (Bodley Head, 1974), p. 196.
11 Machiavelli, *Prince*, pp. 90-1.
12 This sentence is a deliberate imitation of Machiavelli's style; he uses this construction time and again. Renaissance writers loved such imitation and echoes.
13 J.R. Hale (ed.), *The Literary Works of Machiavelli* (OUP, 1961), p. 132.
14 *Ibid*, p. 139.
15 F. Chabod, *Machiavelli and the Renaissance* (Bowes & Bowes, 1958), p. 98.
16 Machiavelli, *Prince*, p. 95.
17 *Ibid*, p. 100.
18 The future Richard III in Shakespeare, *3 Henry VI*, III, 2, 193.
19 Francis Bacon, *The Advancement of Learning* [1605] (Dent, 1915), p. 165.
20 N. Machiavelli, *The Discourses* (Penguin Books, 1970), pp. 277-8.
21 Machiavelli, *Prince*, p. 96.

Answering source-based questions on 'Renaissance Man and the Real World'

1. Federigo da Montefeltro: Soldier and Scholar

Read the two extracts from Vespasiano on page 86 and look at the illustration of the Justus de Ghent portrait on page 85, then answer the following questions:

a) Does the fact that Vespasiano was a bookseller who supplied manuscripts to Federigo for his library make you more or less inclined to value his comments? N.B. You may wish to answer 'both'. Explain the reasons for your answer. (3 marks)

b) Federigo commissioned the portrait from Justus de Ghent: why do you think he wanted to be portrayed in this way? Vespasiano always flattered his subjects: why do you think he believed Federigo would have liked his comments? How are these two questions related and what problems for the historian are inherent in them? (3 marks)

c) How much do Vespasiano's *Life* and Justus's portrait of Federigo tell us about the ideal of the soldier-scholar in Renaissance Italy? (4 marks)

2. *French Invasion of 1494 and the Mercenaries*
Read the extracts from Castiglione, Guicciardini and Machiavelli,
pages 87 and 91, then answer the following questions
a) Why did Castiglione think the Italians were superior to the
French? Why do you think he was able to write in this way over a
decade after the invasion of 1494? How do his two comments on
that invasion on pages 89 and 92 affect your judgement of this? (4
marks)
b) Why did the humanists dislike the mercenaries? How far do the
extracts from Guicciardini and Machiavelli answer that question,
and what do they leave unsaid? (6 marks).

Summary Diagram
Renaissance Man and the Real World

THE IDEAL | **THE REALITY**

| Civic Humanism and Citizen Militias |
| Condottieri and Mercenary Armies |

RENAISSANCE MAN

| Arms and Letters The Soldier-Scholar |
| Italians defeated by the French in 1494 |

| Balance Harmony Universality |
| Machiavelli's *The Prince* *Realpolitik* |

'To Liberate Italy from the Barbarians' ◄── **Machiavelli** ──► New Secular Political Morality

Answering essay questions on 'Renaissance Man and the Real World'

1. '"Renaissance Man" was a scholars' ideal, not a living reality.' Discuss.
2. Why did the French invasion of 1494 have such an effect upon Italian morale?
3. 'Realistic but immoral': examine this view of Machiavelli's political thought.

Both question 1 and question 3 ask you to discuss or examine a statement in quotation marks. Neither of these are 'real' quotations; they were invented for the purpose of the question. This means that they might be deliberately provocative and that you might be wrong to agree fully with them. You need to look critically at quotations and to think deeply about them. It might be right for you to agree with them, or to disagree, or to agree with part and disagree with another part. There is no clue in the wording of the question - you have to think about it. At first sight, you might think you can safely agree with the quotation in question one. The concept of 'Renaissance Man' was an ideal and very few real men were like that. Much of your answer will be concerned with discussing that. But the quotation specifies a *scholars'* ideal and you might want to devote a paragraph to exploring that. Did the notion of 'Renaissance Man' have a wider currency? Clearly, it did not extend to the uneducated in the countryside, but it may have been shared by a wider group of sophisticated urban dwellers, including some painters and sculptors, who were not themselves scholars.

Generally speaking, however, you are likely to end up largely agreeing with the quotation in question 1. But question 3 is very different. Here, the quotation is deliberately provocative. You need to examine each term in turn and apply it to different aspects of Machiavelli's thinking. You could argue that whereas his view of political behaviour was realistic his practical solution to the problems of Italy was not. You could then argue that the way he suggests a prince should behave is immoral from a strictly Christian point of view, but viewed from a broader ethical standpoint it could be argued that it was indeed a moral point of view.

In short, you must approach questions with quotations in them with an open and critical mind. Do not assume that quotations in them will necessarily be true.

8 The Art Business

How many Italian Renaissance artists can you name? Two? Five? Ten? Even if you can manage more than that, you are still identifying only a tiny minority. *The Encyclopaedia of the Italian Renaissance*, edited by John Hale, cites 102 painters, 31 sculptors and 28 architects, but again this is only a small proportion of the total. There was of course an élite, a few leading artists of outstanding talent - the names we all remember; but as significant to the historian as the quality is the sheer quantity of Renaissance artists. For every 'famous' artist, whose work is preserved today in the leading galleries of the world, there were perhaps 100 others who churned out poor quality paintings of the Madonna to be sold in tiny shops as devotional objects. Minor artists would copy the modern styles of the leading masters as best they could, but would also cater for more conservative tastes.

Renaissance Italy is renowned for its art and no book on this subject would be complete without a chapter on it. Specialist works by art historians explore techniques - chiaroscuro (the use of light and shade), contrapposto (the twisting of a body on its axis), perspective, and so on - and trace complex influences over the years. But this book is a general history which seeks to relate Renaissance art to the society which gave rise to it. The two principal aims of this chapter are to show how Renaissance painting and sculpture reflected interests and values of the society and culture that produced it, and to see how awareness of their historical context can illuminate our under-standing of those works of art. Of course the élite is important and a few of the leading artists - Brunelleschi, Masaccio, Donatello, Botticelli, Leonardo, Raphael and Michelangelo - will be discussed in the third and fourth sections of this chapter, but in the first two sections we shall take a broader view of the art business.

1 The Patrons of Art

Renaissance Italy was a commercial society and art was a business. In significant ways the status of the artist rose in this period. Before, artists had been seen largely as craftsmen, like masons and carpenters, but leading Renaissance artists insisted they were akin to scholars and intellectuals and the minor artists benefited to some extent from this new perception. But despite this, they were still producing goods for sale in a market economy. Money lay at the heart of the artistic world. Few men made a fortune from art, but many made a living. It is significant that the art boom of the Renaissance took place in an urban, commercial context and a moneyed society in which capitalist businessmen had surplus cash to dispose of by purchasing works of art. A great deal of recent research has focused attention on the patrons and clients of artists. Patrons are often defined as those who went to an artist and regularly commissioned specific pieces of work, clients as those who commissioned a single piece or wandered into an artist's shop and chose a ready-made painting off the wall.

We can identify at least six major sources of patronage. First, there was the Church. Paintings and sculptures became part of the fabric or furniture of a church. Frescoes were painted directly onto the wall when the plaster was wet and some sculpted stone would be built into the fabric, often around a doorway or into a stone screen. Moveable panel paintings and free-standing statues were important elements of church furniture. Statues were used to focus the devotional thoughts of worshippers, and narrative paintings acted as teaching aids by telling stories to those unable to read. Church money also paid for works of art not in churches; bishops and cardinals had their portraits painted and many popes spent vast sums decorating the Vatican palace. Raphael's *School of Athens* and Michelangelo's ceiling of the Sistine Chapel (see the illustrations on pages 115 and 119), both painted for Julius II, are just two examples of papal patronage. Secondly, in some cities, pre-eminently in Florence, the guilds were

Florence Cathedral, from the palace of the signoria, showing Brunelleschi's cupola

major patrons. As well as decorating their guildhalls, most of the Florentine guilds commissioned a statue for one of the niches of Orsanmichele (see page 27). The cloth guild took special responsibility for the Baptistery of Florence Cathedral and in 1401 they sponsored a competition for a design for a huge pair of bronze doors depicting stories from the Bible. Not to be outdone, in 1418 the Wool Guild, which looked after the Cathedral itself, announced a competition for a design for a cupola (or dome). The competition was won by the Florentine architect, Brunelleschi, and the cupola he produced, illustrated on page 102, was the object of wonder and admiration.

Thirdly, some individuals purchased works of art. While people of relatively modest means could be clients of minor artists buying ready-made pictures from their shops, one needed to be wealthy to commission a work from a major artist. Great families might become patrons to mark occasions like marriages; individuals might have their portrait painted once in their lifetime for their family to treasure. Fourthly, some who were not rich enough to commission works as individuals were able to do so as part of a confraternity (see page 33). Often a confraternity would commission a panel painting for the altar of their side chapel in the parish church; on ceremonial days they would carry this painting through the streets of the city as part of a great procession. Fifthly, communal governments were patrons. Works of art were prestigious and the honour of the city required that its public rooms and squares were decorated with paintings and sculptures from leading artists - if possible, sons of the city. When, after the death of Savonarola, Florence sought to make her constitution more like that of Venice, a large room in the palace of the *signoria* was designated to act like the Venetian Hall of the Great Council and two huge frescoes were commissioned, one by Leonardo the other by Michelangelo. The latter was never painted; the former decayed after only a few years as Leonardo had experimented with a new fresco technique which did not work. In Venice the paintings in the Doge's Palace were frequently updated and replaced so that the most modern work was always on show to impress visitors.

Sixthly, there was court patronage; when a city was ruled by a prince, patronage took rather a different form. Instead of the government commissioning individual works from artists, a court painter would enter the employment of the prince and be available constantly to do whatever was needed. The Gonzagas at Mantua wanted to lure the leading painter Andrea Mantegna away from Padua into their court, so offered him '15 ducats a month, the provision of rooms where you can live with your family, enough food each year to feed six, [and] enough firewood for your use'.[1] A position as court painter gave an artist security, but limited his freedom. If his patron had good taste, an artist could be given time and opportunity to establish his reputation, but the death of a prince might suddenly leave him with an unreasonable patron - a man like Galeazzo Maria Sforza in Milan who sometimes 'wanted a room to be decorated with the noblest figures in a single night'.[2]

Why did Renaissance people spend their money on works of art? Motives varied, but five reasons recur. First and foremost was piety - works of art glorified God and led men and women to worship and devotion. Then there was the honour of the city or the state and thirdly the prestige of the family or the prince. Next there was 'the pleasure and virtue of spending money well'; if profit had been made by doubtful means, such as usury, the patronage of religious works in particular could help clear the conscience. Lastly, there was simply the delight of owning things of good quality; one man described art for its own sake as 'a voluptuous pleasure as when a man is in love'.[3] Although this was a commercial society, works of art were valued for themselves and the prestige they conferred, they were not seen as financial investments. In Renaissance Italy men and women did not buy paintings in order to resell them at a profit.

2 Patrons, Artists and Workshops

a) Contracts between Patrons and Artists

Patrons were, then, important in the social and economic context of the art business, but how much did they affect what the work of art itself would look like? As in other areas of life, such as marriage or the employment of mercenaries, a detailed contract was signed by both sides. This would usually specify the subject matter, often in considerable detail. In the case of a narrative series of frescoes, which (for example) told the life-story of a saint, the subject of each picture would be specified. Often the contract would include a drawing, or in the case of sculpture a small model, which illustrated the agreed form of the work. Contracts also frequently referred to the materials to be used. In specifying the quality and cost of certain paints, the patron indirectly dictated some of the colours of the work. Traditionally, the Virgin Mary is shown in a blue gown. This was because blue was the most expensive pigment and it would have dishonoured her to use a different colour. To be more specific, Mary wore ultramarine azure made from the semi-precious stone lapis-lazuli, imported from the east. This was ground to a fine powder, then soaked in a mixture of pine rosin, gum and wax.[4] The first pressing of this produced a rich violet blue; later soakings and pressings (rather like using a tea bag for the second or third time) produced weaker colours. The use of gold leaf, usually as a background, was often specified, although, as the Renaissance progressed, gold was used less and less. The skill of the artist, in painting an imaginary background, came to be valued more than the use of expensive materials and only the more conservative patrons continued to insist on the use of gold. Contracts often specified the price and date of delivery of a piece. Like other commercial contracts, the cost of the work and how this was to be paid was clearly set out. How the price was determined could affect the quality of the work. Those who (like the boorish Borso d'Este, Duke of Ferrara) paid by the square foot got a different product from those connoisseurs who paid the artist for his time and his materials. Court painters had, of course, a regular salary and were not paid for individual works. Otherwise, payment was often by instalments to ensure that the work was finished. Delivery dates were specified and sometimes an artist promised he would work on nothing else until the piece was completed. Penalty clauses might provide for compensation if the work deteriorated too soon. In 1445 the Tuscan painter Piero della Francesca promised 'to restore at his own expense every blemish

Benozzo: Madonna with Saints, *National Gallery, London.*

which the said picture may show in the course of time for the next ten years, on account either of the defect of the wood or of the said Piero'.[5] Artists usually employed assistants who would paint the less important parts of the picture, so contracts often specified which figures the master must do himself.

Just how detailed the control would be is shown by this contract for a painting by Benozzo Gozzoli now in the National Gallery in London (see the illustration on page 105, or better still go and look at the painting itself, if you can). Benozzo was not in the first rank of painters and this is not one of the 'great' works of the period, but he was a competent Florentine artist whose patrons included the Medici and whose work is much more typical of the art business as a whole than that of the few exceptionally talented geniuses whose names we all know. In 1461 Benozzo signed a contract with a Florentine confraternity which illustrates many of the points made above. The representatives of the confraternity chosen to deal with him were a linen merchant, a shoemaker, a mercer (a dealer in textiles) and a notary (lawyer) - each a 'worthy Florentine citizen'. They insisted that Benozzo should do the work himself, in his best style and set out in detail the images to be depicted:

> 1 First, in the middle of the said picture, the figure of Our Lady on the throne, in the manner and form and with the same decorations as the picture above the High Altar in San Marco, Florence. And on the right-hand side of the picture, beside Our Lady, the figure of St John the
> 5 Baptist in his accustomed clothing, and beside him the figure of St Zenobius in pontifical vestments; and then the figure of St Jerome kneeling, with his usual emblems, and on the left-hand side the following saints: first, beside Our Lady, the figure of St Peter, and beside him St Dominic, and by St Dominic the figure of St Francis kneeling, with every
> 10 customary ornament... And all the azure used for the picture must be very fine azure... And on the other hand, the said Domenico promises in their name to pay the said Benozzo for all his expenses, gold, gesso [the plaster of Paris surface which was used to paint on] and colours, 300 lire ... 100 lire to be paid at present, and 80 lire in six months from
> 15 now, and the rest of the sum when the said painting is finished; and to have this, the said Benozzo must furnish everything by the beginning of November next year at latest.[6]

b) Artists and their Workshops

Contracts such as this give us an insight into workshop practices and to understand them we need to consider the environment in which most artists worked. The word 'workshop' had several meanings. First, it was the place where the work of art was manufactured and the tools and equipment necessary for this process were housed. Secondly, it was the business office where the artist met his patrons and where works were commissioned. Thirdly, it was a place for the training of young artists; even the leading artists of the future, like Donatello, Botticelli, Leonardo and Michelangelo, received their early training in the workshops of older, more traditional artists. Lastly, it was the group of people - assistants and apprentices - who worked for the master-artist, and who together with him produced the paintings to which he gave his name. Each workshop had its own style and expertise; some specialised in fresco or panel painting, others in bronze-work or stone.

Workshops often produced their own materials - pens and charcoal, pigments and paints. Brushes for the rougher work were made from the bristles of domestic hogs (the white was considered better than the black); for finer work brushes of miniver tails (or ermine) were used. Frames were normally purchased from a specialist woodworker and artists often acquired the frame before painting the picture. Wooden panels for painting were made smooth with a thin layer of plaster of Paris (*gesso*). Some colours were purchased from specialist producers, others made in the workshop. In his handbook for craftsmen, Cennini recommended a slab of red porphyry as the hardest stone on which to grind colours; his description of the process suggests long hours of tedious work for apprentices:

1   take a portion of this black, or of any other color, the size of a nut; and put it on this stone, and with the (other stone) which you hold in your hand crush this black up thoroughly. Then take some clear river or fountain or well water, and grind this black for the space of half an hour, or
5   an hour, or as long as you like; but know that if you were to work it up for a year it would be so much the blacker and better a color.[7]

The walls of a modern art gallery divorce Renaissance paintings from the various contexts for which they were produced. Artists' workshops manufactured goods for a wide range of purposes: some were for altar-pieces, others for wedding chests; some were part of the interior design scheme of a private home, others were for the state rooms of a court or a constitutional meeting place. Portraits might be for domestic delight or political propaganda. Workshops understood these contexts and purposes and they adapted the style accordingly. Art was part of the everyday life of Renaissance urban society; it was produced in a bustling workshop, to be enjoyed in home, office and church. It was a major industry. In 25 years one single workshop produced 400 works of art[8]; in Florence alone there might have been around 200 workshops. The 'famous' paintings by the élite of 'great' artists, which are considered in the next two sections, were only a tip of an iceberg, and it is important to think of them in this wider context.

3 The Art of the Early Renaissance

But this élite mattered. Artists are regarded as great and works become famous because of their ability and quality; they mark important advances in the development of art. When in the sixteenth century Giorgio Vasari, friend and pupil of Michelangelo, came to write the first history of Renaissance art in his *Lives of the Artists*, he set out to depict it as a steady progress, advancing ever upwards from the 'weak' art of the Middle Ages to the 'absolute perfection' of Michelangelo.[9] He soon ran into trouble as it became apparent that some of the early Renaissance artists were 'better' than some of the later ones. Vasari never resolved this problem because he never abandoned his idea of *progress*; modern historians are happier with the word *development*. While we can trace important lines of change through Renaissance art, we cannot say that Michelangelo is better than Donatello, or Raphael better than Masaccio. This section and the next will outline the most important of these developments by considering a few of the leading artists and discussing a handful of their works. It is not that these artists are necessarily the best or these works the only important ones, but because they illustrate the evolution of art in this period. Many other paintings could equally well have been discussed instead; these are samples of the evidence which, as historians, we must examine.

There are three important things you must bear in mind as you read the following accounts. First, things changed over time: this section deals with the Early Renaissance up to the 1490s; the next section is on the ensuing High Renaissance. Secondly, artistic styles differed in various places; not only were towns like Urbino and Perugia less 'up-to-date' than Florence and Rome, but also cities like Venice, Milan and Naples developed distinctive styles of their own, different from, not worse than, that of Florence. Thirdly, the three major branches of the visual arts - painting, sculpture and architecture - were all closely linked; developments in one influenced the others and some individuals worked in two or even three of these branches.

A problem which faced Vasari and still faces the historian today is to know where to begin. For a long time, old and new styles existed alongside each other. We can see traces of the new ideas by the early fourteenth century in the work of Giotto whose painting of the human body was influenced by his study of the sculpture of his day. He had a fine dramatic eye and could take a Bible tale and depict one moment in that story which encapsulated both the critical point of the narrative and a spiritual and psychological insight into the characters. His work exerted an immense influence on fifteenth-century Italian artists, but the Black Death, which hit Italy ten years after his death, may have arrested artistic change for perhaps two generations. Certainly the next major development took place in Florence early in the fifteenth century. An exciting artistic climate of experiment and innovation led to major breakthroughs in the 1420s when the architect Brunelleschi, the painter Masaccio and the sculptor Donatello were all working there. The connections between the three friends and the three branches of art they represented were as important as their individual achievements.

a) Filippo Brunelleschi (1377-1446)

Brunelleschi turned to architecture after losing the competition for the Baptistery doors. His design for the Innocenti Hospital, built to house the city's orphans, thrilled people with its elegant newness and its echoes of the classical past. The pointed arches of the Middle Ages were replaced by semi-circular ones, a whole row of which gives access from the hospital's loggia (or open-arcade) to the piazza; the windows had triangular pediments above them. His most famous achievement was to design and superintend the building of the cupola of Florence Cathedral (see page 103 and the illustration on page 102). For 50 years Florentines had wanted to build a dome over the 140 feet (43 metres) wide space at the crossing of the cathedral, but no one had the necessary engineering skills. When Brunelleschi solved the problem in the 1420s, a fellow Florentine artist rejoiced in:

1 such an enormous construction towering above the skies, vast enough to cover the entire Tuscan population with its shadow, and done without the aid of beams or elaborate wooden supports. Surely a feat of engineering ... that people did not believe possible these days and was
5 probably equally unknown and unimaginable among the ancients.[10]

Brunelleschi also developed a theory of artificial perspective which allowed a painter to represent three dimensional objects on a flat surface in a convincing way. This involved establishing a single point - the vanishing point of the perspective - where all lines drawn at right-angles to the surface of the painting would meet, or, to put it another way, the point where all parallel lines would *appear* to converge as they recede into the distance. Foreshortening of parts of the picture created an impression of distance and depth. Artists delighted in floors with rectangular paving stones or tiles which enabled them to show off their skill in perspective (see the illustrations on pages 63 and 115). But much depended on viewers of the painting standing in the right place and keeping their heads still, and it has been argued that perspective was developed as much to control the observer as to create illusions.

b) Masaccio (1401-c.1428)

One of the many painters to experiment with perspective in the early days was Brunelleschi's friend, Masaccio who died young and whose immense reputation is founded on three works. One of these was an

Masaccio, Tribute Money, St. Maria del Carmine, Florence

altar-piece for a church in Pisa, the central part of which is now in the National Gallery in London. Another was a painting of the Trinity in the church of Santa Maria Novella in Florence. Although painted on a flat wall, this gives the impression of the figures standing in front of a small side chapel built in the most modern of styles with a barrel-vaulted ceiling painted in accurate perspective and giving a wonderful illusion of depth. It was rumoured that Brunelleschi designed this ceiling for his friend to paint. But, perhaps the most influential of all Masaccio's works were his frescoes in the Brancacci Chapel in the Carmelite church on the other side of the river Arno. In *The Tribute Money*, which is shown on page 110, the head of Christ is at the vanishing point on which all the lines of perspective converge; on the right a building and on the left countryside are part of this perspective scheme which provides a real space for the figures to inhabit.

The whole of the action takes place within this unified space, but three separate moments in time are shown; later paintings would depict a single instant. In the central part of the fresco, the tax collector demands money from Christ and the apostles; Christ tells St Peter to take from the lake a fish, in the mouth of which is a coin for the tribute, and on the left of the painting we see St Peter doing so; on the right, he is shown handing the tribute money to the tax collector. Instead of flooding the picture with light from all directions as was usual, Masaccio imagined a single source of light coming from the right and throwing consistent shadows. Christ and the apostles are shown as figures of great dignity, dressed like ancient Roman senators, unlike the tax gatherer who wears contemporary doublet and hose. The figures convince us they are real because Masaccio has imagined skeletons with muscles determining the way their robes fall. Facial expressions show psychological insight, seriousness and dignity of purpose. Masaccio gives us the most convincing representation of real people in real space, and it is small wonder that artists flocked from all over Italy to see this work.

c) Donatello (1386-1466)

Masaccio's painting of the human figure was much influenced by his study of contemporary sculpture; the leading sculptor of the early Renaissance, Donatello, was another of his friends. Donatello worked in both marble and bronze; the techniques were very different. Whereas a statue in marble, like his St George for the niche of the Armourers guild on Orsanmichele, was carved from the stone with hammer and chisel, a bronze would first be built up in clay, covered in wax on which the fine details of the surface would be cut, then covered again with an outer casing of clay. The layer of wax would then be removed by melting and the space filled with molten bronze. No one had cast a life-size, free-standing, nude figure in bronze since classical times and Donatello's *David*, illustrated on page 117, was hailed as a great feat of engineering as well as a remarkable work of art. Donatello represented David not as the old king, as had become common in the Middle Ages, but as the youth who killed Goliath. To depict him nude was to take on a great challenge: clothing could hide a sculptor's lack of anatomical command; nudes demanded a complete knowledge of the skeleton and muscles of the human body. Such was Donatello's mastery that contemporaries wondered if it had been modelled not in clay but on the living form of a boy's body. The statue was remarkable not only for the skill in casting it, and for the anatomical accuracy, but also for its psychological insight. It has a sensuous cruelty which is chilling to see. With his foot on the severed head of Goliath, leaning languidly on his sword, one feels this beautiful boy has enjoyed the act of killing.

Unlike Masaccio, Donatello lived to an old age and produced a large body of work. The rest of it - much less disturbing than the *David* - included a huge bronze of the mercenary captain *Gattamelata* astride a massive horse, a number of Madonnas, crucifixions and saints for churches and a heart-rending woodcarving of St Mary Magdalene in penitence. Donatello played a crucial part alongside Brunelleschi and Masaccio in the trio who transformed the visual arts in the 1420s, then lived on to dominate fifteenth-century sculpture.

d) Sandro Botticelli (1445-1510)

Between 1430 and 1490, painting continued to develop. In some ways, figures became more real, more human. Take the use of the halo for instance. In early works the halo was shown like a large dinner plate, flat behind the saint's head. Then the plate was shown hovering above the head in perspective and soon the plate became a hoop, before it was finally dispensed with altogether. But in other ways, realism reached a peak with Masaccio's generation; subsequently other things became more important to the painter, such as the symbolic and allegorical meaning of the work. Botticelli was an artist from a later generation who illustrates this point well. Although perfectly capable of painting anatomy accurately, at times he distorts the proportions of the human body to achieve other effects.

He learned his trade in Florentine artists' workshops as a fellow apprentice of Filippino Lippi (see cover) and Leonardo da Vinci. He was influenced by Neoplatonist philosophy and in a series of masterpieces painted in the 1470s and 1480s he explored those ideas in a number of symbolic paintings. Best known is his painting of *The Birth of Venus*, an elongated nude figure, blown in from the sea on a large scallop shell, but possibly even more important was his *Primavera* - the allegory of Spring - illustrated on page 113. More has been written about this painting than any other Renaissance work of art. Although there is no real agreement on the painting's meaning, most scholars believe it is deeply symbolic. One popular Neoplatonic reading suggests that the theme of the painting is Platonic Love (see pages 76-7). At its centre is the figure of Venus, her hand raised to invite us into her kingdom. She is pregnant and the whole painting is, like the Spring, full of fruitfulness and new life. Above her head, her son the blindfolded Cupid fires an arrow at the figures of the Three Graces, a traditional theme of classical art, who represent here the three stages of Platonic Love - sensual, spiritual and divine. Divine Love, in the centre of the group, her hands entwined with those of both her sisters, is gazing at the god Mercury at the left of the picture, who points the way to heaven. So, beauty and love lead us to God. Other interpretations stress the influence of the Roman poets Ovid and Lucretius with their allegories of spring and suggest that the three figures on the right are (from right to left) Zephyr, Chloris and Flora. Zephyr, the god of the west wind, rapes Chloris, a nymph of the bare earth, causing flowers to spring from her mouth and transforming her into Flora, the goddess of flowers and gardens, 'scattering the blossoms gathered in the fold of her garment onto the path before her'.[11] Whatever the precise explanation, the important point to remember is that Botticelli is using a painting to say something profound about the nature of human existence. The rebirth of nature

Botticelli: Primavera, *Uffizi, Florence*

in Spring, sexual fecundity, the portrayal of love and the way to God are all brought together in this picture, which draws on a range of classical traditions and presents their wisdom to the Christian world.

4 The Art of the High Renaissance

The terms Early Renaissance and High Renaissance have become convenient labels, but they are imprecise terms and are identified as much by place as time. The artistic achievements of the High Renaissance started in Florence sometime in the 1490s and flourished in Rome in the first two or three decades of the sixteenth century during the pontificates of Julius II (1503-13) and Leo X (1513-21); Leonardo, Raphael and Michelangelo were its major figures.

a) Leonardo da Vinci (1452-1519)

Leonardo's reputation and influence was much greater than the body of work he completed. Almost as important as his paintings are his notebooks and drawings (see the illustration on page 85). The range of his interests was immense and it may seem churlish to regret that these distracted him from painting in which he was a true master and promised so much more than he achieved. He lived to be almost 70, but all we have is about a dozen paintings - 'about' because the attribution of some is disputed. He trained in a workshop in Florence and his earliest work is an angel he contributed to a *Baptism of Christ* by his master Verrochio. In Milan, he painted a revolutionary *Last Supper* on the wall of the monks' refectory at Santa Maria delle Grazie, and two very similar versions of *The Virgin of the Rocks*, one now in Paris, the other in London - the rocky background, by the way, was demanded in the contract by the confraternity which commissioned it. In Florence, he painted outstanding portraits of Ginevra Benci and Mona Lisa and, perhaps his masterpiece, the *Virgin and St Anne*. Here, the Virgin sits on her mother's knee and leans forward to restrain the infant Christ who is reaching out to embrace a lamb which, as contemporaries recognised, represented his passion and death.

b) Raphael (1483-1520)

The change in focus of the High Renaissance from Florence to Rome is well illustrated by the career of Raphael. He was a painter of frescoes and panel paintings, of classical and of religious subjects, and the leading portrait painter of the period. What is remarkable, when looking through the large body of work he produced, is how radically his style changed depending on where he was and which other painters were influencing him at the time. This is not to suggest that he copied other people's styles in a slavish way, rather that he was always open to new ideas which he made his own. He came from the

Raphael: Detail of The School of Athens, *Vatican. Plato, on the left, a portrait of Leonardo da Vinci, is holding his dialogue* Timaeus, *Aristotle holds his discourse* Ethics

Raphael: The Wedding of the Virgin, *Milan, Brera*

provinces - Urbino, up in the hills - and his early works are old fashioned and provincial in style. In *The Wedding of the Virgin* (1504), illustrated on page 115, the artist shows off all his early skills. While Mary and Joseph, with their serene group of well-behaved guests, dominate the foreground, behind them, beyond a geometrically paved piazza, stands an ideal Renaissance building looking just like an illustration in an architectural textbook. When Raphael came to Florence in 1504, and saw the work of Leonardo and the Florentine masters, his style changed dramatically, but it was after his arrival in Rome in 1508 that he reached his maturity. He established himself as the leading painter of the High Renaissance; papal Rome was the setting of his triumph. His arrival there coincided with Michelangelo starting work on the ceiling of the Sistine Chapel, which is part of the Vatican Palace. As Michelangelo painted the ceiling, just a few dozen yards away Raphael was decorating the walls of the papal apartments with a series of remarkable frescoes which were much influenced by what he had seen of Michelangelo's work. In 1511, the year in which the scaffolding was removed from the Sistine Chapel, Raphael completed his painting of the nearby Stanza della Segnatura, including the large fresco of *The School of Athens*. This depicted the leading Athenian philosophers, scientists and mathematicians and included hidden portraits of Leonardo as Plato (see the illustration on page 115) and of Michelangelo.

c) Michelangelo (1475-1564)

Whilst we should certainly reject Vasari's idea of progress in Renaissance art, it is difficult not to agree with him that Michelangelo was the outstanding genius of the period. Also a master in the arts of architecture and painting, Michelangelo was first and foremost a sculptor in marble. He was industrious and prolific, working solidly for 73 years from his first marble in 1491, at the age of 16, to his final day's carving less than a week before his death at the age of almost 89. As an architect his most important work was that on St Peter's Rome, the mother church of Catholicism, and no one can fully understand Michelangelo's work who does not recognise that his intense Catholic faith was a major influence upon it. He was also a poet who, as well as producing a series of intense love sonnets, also reflected on his work:

> The best of artists never has a concept
> A single marble block does not contain
> Inside its husk, but to it may attain
> Only if hand follows the intellect.[12]

Michelangelo's work is profoundly intellectual; just as a scholar worked in words, so he worked in marble or paint. He much preferred marble, producing around 40 works in that medium.

Right: Michelangelo,
David, *Accademia,*
Florence.
Marble 410 centimetres
(13 ft 6 in.) 1501-4

Below: Donatello, David,
Bargello, Florence. Bronze
158 centimetres (5 ft 2 in.)

The sculpture which established his reputation in Florence was the huge marble *David*, illustrated on page 117, which he carved between 1501 and 1504. The figure alone, without its base, is 13 feet 6 inches (410 centimetres) high. It was placed outside the palace of the *signoria*, just a few hundred yards from the house where he was born, and it is indeed the work of a Florentine patriot. Facing south towards Rome, which then posed a potential threat to Florentine liberty, it depicted David, not after Goliath was dead as Donatello had done, but looking out warily for his enemy, ready to face whatever came. This monumental, defiant nude, reminiscent of, but not the same as, the statues of the Ancient World, may appear to us as a pagan work, glorifying man not God. But that would be to misunderstand both Michelangelo's faith and Renaissance thinking. In representing the perfection of the human body, Michelangelo was celebrating what he believed to be God's greatest creation. Here classicism and Christianity came together. The work is full of symbols and ideas. Take, for instance, the way he depicts the right and left hand sides of the body and compare this to the painted figure of Adam on the Sistine ceiling, illustrated on page 119. In each case, the right-hand side, known as the solar side, is closed like a curved defensive wall around a city; the left, the lunar, is open and vulnerable but also more creative; together the two sides of the body show the complexity of humankind. Ten years later he carved a marble figure of Moses: the right-hand side is solid, Moses clutches firmly the tablets with the Ten Commandments - the definitive law; the left is full of movement as if the prophet is about to stand, perhaps to attempt to lead his people out of Egypt. In all three works, it is the right-hand side of the body which bears the figure's weight, the left which has the potential for hazardous action.

Michelangelo was a reluctant painter, forced to the task by the insistence of powerful popes who would not take no for an answer. Apart from a small circular painting of the Holy Family, commissioned by a Florentine businessman early in his career and a couple of late minor works, Michelangelo did only two paintings in his lifetime, but both were massive. From 1508 to 1512 he painted the ceiling of the Sistine Chapel for Pope Julius II, then from 1536-1541 he returned to the Sistine Chapel to paint *The Last Judgement* on the wall behind the altar for Pope Paul III. The details of the ceiling are full of symbolism and will repay close study, but even more important is the scheme of the whole work. For once, the subject matter was left to the artist. He divided the centre of the ceiling into nine panels, four large ones alternating with five small ones, showing in chronological order scenes from Genesis from the story of the creation to Noah. The illustration on page 119 shows a section of this. Each of the small panels was surrounded by four naked male youths who symbolise the classical world, and this Neoplatonic union of classical and Christian is further emphasised by the figures on either side. Here he alternated

Michelangelo: Detail of the Sistine Chapel Ceiling, 1508-12: The large panel shows the creation of Adam, the small panels the separation of the land from the water and the creation of Eve. Each of the small panels is surrounded by four nude youths. To the left of the separation of the land and water we have the classical Persian sibyl, to the right the Old Testament prophet Daniel; to the right of the creation of Eve is the pagan Cumaean sibyl, to its left the Biblical figure of Ezekiel

five Old Testament prophets and five pagan Roman sibyls whose prophecies were believed to have foretold the birth of Christ. So, at the very heart of Christendom, in the Pope's private chapel, Michelangelo brought together the classical and the Christian worlds. There is no more potent symbol of Renaissance thinking.

5 Conclusion

Renaissance art reflected the beliefs and preoccupations of the society which produced it. It drew on both classical and Christian traditions. It placed human beings at the centre of its vision of the world. It was concerned with balance and symmetry, with order and imagination. Just as the early Renaissance humanists were preoccupied with the precision of the Latin language and with the removal of anachronisms from texts so that they could see the Ancient World clearly, so Masaccio and Donatello sought to represent real people in real space; accurate representation provided insights into the nature of humanity. Later in the fifteenth and early sixteenth centuries, as Neoplatonist ideas became more influential, so Botticelli and Michelangelo produced work richer in symbolism, in which the ideas behind the composition were as important as its visual impact. Works like the Sistine ceiling are a microcosm of the complex relationship between Renaissance Italy and the Ancient World. Artists were not alone responsible for the ideas enshrined in their work. Patrons were often explicit in their requirements and contracts frequently spelled out the subject matter and iconography of a painting or of a piece of sculpture in detail. Rich men who were the patrons both of artists and scholars, sometimes used the scholars' knowledge of Greek and Latin myths to establish a programme for artists to paint or sculpt. To understand the meaning of Italian Renaissance art one must place it not just in the practical context of the workshop, but also the intellectual world of their patrons - of Christianity and of humanist scholarship.

References

1 D.S. Chambers, *Patrons and Artists in the Italian Renaissance* (Macmillan, 1970), p. 117.
2 *Ibid*, p. 154.
3 P. Burke, *Tradition and Innovation in Renaissance Italy* (Fontana, 1974), p. 107.
4 Cennini, *The Craftsman's Handbook* (Dover Publications, 1933/1960), pp. 36-9.
5 Chambers, *Patrons and Artists*, p. 53.
6 *Ibid*, pp. 54-5.
7 Cennini, *Craftsman's Handbook*, p. 21.
8 A.Thomas, *The Painter's Practice in Renaissance Tuscany* (Cambridge University Press, 1995).

9   Vasari, *The Lives of the Artists* vol. 1 (Penguin Books, 1965), p. 325.
10 Leon Battista Alberti, *On Painting* [1435] (Penguin Books, 1991), p. 35.
11 Charles Dempsey, *The Portrayal of Love: Botticelli's Primavera and Humanist Culture at the Time of Lorenzo the Magnificent* (Princeton, University Press, 1997), p. 30.
12 Michelangelo, *Complete Poems and Selected Letters* (Vintage Books, 1970), p. 100.

Summary Diagram
The Art Business

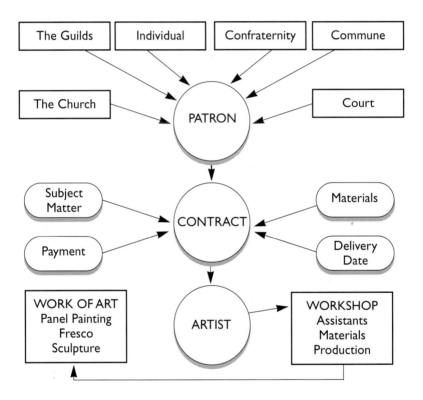

When you have read this chapter, find some of your fellow students who are studying Art and try to explain to them, in your own words, the main ideas you have learned here. Encourage them to ask you questions about it, and think about how these could be answered.

Answering source-based questions on 'The Art Business'

1. Painters and their patrons

Look at the reproduction of the painting by Benozzo on page 105 and the extract from the contract for it on page 106, then answer the following questions.

a) How closely did Benozzo follow the scheme of subject matter set out in the contract and in which major way did he depart from it? (5 marks)

b) What is the significance of the references to materials in the contract? (5 marks)

c) See if you can find out what St Jerome's 'usual emblems' (line 7) were, why emblems were significant, and what 'emblem books' were. (10 marks) N.B. You will not be able to answer this question from the information in this book, so head for the library now. You might start by looking up 'emblem' in the largest dictionary you can find.

Answering essay questions on 'The Art Business'

1. In what ways did the system of patronage affect works of art in Renaissance Italy?

2. How did the economic and social context in which they worked affect artists in Renaissance Italy?

3. Assess the importance of the 1420s in the development of the artistic life of Florence with special reference to the paintings of Masaccio, the architecture of Brunelleschi and the sculptures of Donatello.

4. How did Neoplatonic ideas affect the works of Botticelli and Michelangelo?

When you set out to discuss a work of art, try to be positive, precise and objective. Say what its qualities are. Try to avoid using the word 'famous' to describe a painting. When you use that adjective, all you are saying is that a lot of people today know about the painting. This may be an interesting comment on the values and taste of the present day, but it does not actually tell you anything significant about the painting itself in its Renaissance setting. If you say, on the other hand, that this is an important painting in the history of art because it was one of the first to use perspective in a convincing way, that a sculpture was the first life-size nude figure cast in bronze since classical times, then you are making a significant point. If you can link it to other works of art of the same period, or to the ideas of the humanist scholars, then all the better. Always try to explain the reasons for the importance and significance of works. Just to say that they are 'famous' is to lack both meaning and style.

𝟗 Conclusion

1 The Unity of Renaissance History

It is traditional to end a book with a chapter called the conclusion. If the book is a thriller or murder mystery, then 'conclusion' means the final result or the outcome - the answer to the puzzle or the resolution of the problem. You may hope that a book like this gives you a simple answer to the question 'What was the Renaissance?'. To say that it was 'the interaction and combination of all of the themes analysed in the previous chapters of this book' may disappoint you - but only those of you who think History is a simple subject to study. Serious students know that it is as complicated as life itself. How then can this chapter help you to appreciate the nature of this complexity? Some conclusions seek to summarise what has gone before. But if a summary is no more than a re-capitulation of the chief points made in the book, then the notes you have taken will serve just as well. As Renaissance scholars would have been well aware, the word *summary* comes from a Latin root; an alternative is *synopsis* which derives from the Greek meaning 'general view'. The adjective which comes from this is *synoptic*, which means seeing things together (syn-optic). If we bring together the main points of all the chapters of this book, will this synoptic view reveal to us more than just the sum of its parts?

It has often been said that 'history is a seamless garment': there are few abrupt changes; new periods, like the Renaissance, are woven into the fabric of the past. But there is another way to interpret that saying which seems peculiarly appropriate to Renaissance Italy. There are no seams either between the categories historians impose on the past - economic, social, political, religious, intellectual, cultural and so on. Renaissance Italy has to be seen as a unity and although those divisions may help historians to order their material, they are artificial. After we have analysed the past into such categories and understood them, we then have to put the pieces together again in a synthesis, to try to reconstruct the complete picture of the age. It is the combination and interaction of all these various aspects which make up the totality of Renaissance Italy. All the way through, this book has tried to show the *connections* between the economic, social, political, religious, intellectual and cultural aspects of the period. Each of these has been examined in a separate chapter, and it is the relationship between them which constitutes what we mean by 'Renaissance'.

Human beings lived complex lives which incorporated all of these aspects - they did not keep them in watertight compartments. How people thought or acted in certain areas of their life influenced their behaviour in others. A merchant who was used in his business to striking deals which were financially explicit and legally binding, would approach the negotiations for a marriage contract, either as bridegroom or as father of the bride, in much the same way. When he came to commission a painting from an artist, either for his family or for a confraternity he belonged to, or when, as one of the governors of his city, he came to employ mercenary soldiers to defend the state, those same skills would be employed in drawing up the contract. Hence, his concern with money and with legally binding agreements could be seen in far more than just the economic sphere of his life. In the same way a dowry might have important economic repercussions for the father who paid it and the husband who received it. It was of social importance because it played a central role in marriage negotiations. For a wife it might be a security she carried with her into a marriage, knowing that if she was left a widow she could reclaim it. For a daughter it might be the barrier which prevented her marriage if her father could not raise the sum which the honour of the family required. It could have religious implications for the health of the Church if the lack of it led to unwilling girls being cast into nunneries when they had no desire to live the religious life. It might have significant political consequences if it established an alliance between powerful families in a state.

The connections between the economic, social, political and religious affairs discussed in Chapters two, three, four and five are clear to see. But the interaction did not stop there. The activities of the scholars and artists discussed in Chapters six, seven and eight were also intimately related to the society in which they lived. Scholars and artists depended on patrons for their money and these might be political figures (either princes or the communes of republics), religious ones (popes and prelates), or wealthy individuals - the heads of mighty families who made their fortune in trade, manufacture or banking. Humanist scholars studied Greek and Latin texts and this led them, for example, to give advice to mercenary soldiers (albeit bad advice which was disregarded), or to write histories according to the models of the Ancient World, which were used as propaganda by their political patrons. Men who had the wealth and leisure to pursue an interest in the ideas and the myths of the Ancient World would often commission works of art which reflected those interests - a marble statue of Bacchus, the Roman god of wine, from Michelangelo, or a *Primavera* from Botticelli. The Christian faith also inspired numerous works of art: Masaccio's *Trinity* is a profound meditation on the theology of death and judgement, Donatello's *Magdalene* on repentance and forgiveness. Religion also played a political and sociological role; it was used by princes to justify their rule and to keep the poor in obedience. This list could become a long one, but the point is perhaps already made: each aspect of life abutted and affected every other. Historians analyse and compartmentalise, but real life is messier and more complex than that.

2 Conflict: Classical and Christian

Taking a synoptic view of Renaissance Italy involves us in more than just listing similarities and establishing connections. It also helps us to see more clearly than we can in a single chapter some of the essential conflicts and contradictions of the age. At the heart of the Renaissance lay a major conflict which many contemporaries concealed rather than resolved: Machiavelli exposed it remorselessly and Savonarola was acutely conscious of it but Michelangelo gloried in its ambiguities. The Renaissance brought into a new relationship the classical civilisation of pagan Greece and Rome and the Christian faith of medieval Europe. Renaissance humanists hoped that the wisdom of the Ancient World could combine with the spiritual insight of Christianity to give them a new understanding of mankind and society. To an extent it did, but it also brought a clash of fundamental values, a conflict of interests.

The papacy was the heir of the Roman Empire; the Romans had been the inheritors of the Greeks. The word *Rome* therefore represents both classical civilization and the Christian Church. Compared to the life of a great nation, Christianity was at once both smaller and vaster. It was small scale in that it evolved as a code of personal behaviour for the individual living in a tiny community; it was vast in its claim to explain the whole of history in four stages, from Creation, Fall (of Adam and Eve), Atonement (of Christ on the cross) to Judgement (at the end of the world). The classical civilisations of Greece and Rome, however, took a different view of human nature and public life. Aristotle argued that man was 'by nature a political animal'.[1] The Ancient World evolved a philosophy for a political community, a nation state, an empire, which recognised man's acquisitiveness and passions, and valued his boldness and aggression. From the conversion of the Emperor Constantine to the present day these two incompatible strains have co-existed in uncomfortable union. Civic humanists, like Leonardo Bruni, used the example of the Roman Republic to advocate the active participation of the leading citizens in the government of their state, and his *History of Florence*, modelled on ancient histories of Rome, encouraged feelings of patriotism. Machiavelli was denounced and ignored when he set out clearly the incompatibility between Christianity and government and exposed how much political life depended on the pagan tradition of the Ancient World. Machiavelli was able to see what most of his contemporaries could not because he was prepared to step outside of the Christian world-view and so was able to see it in perspective. But some of those who remained firmly within the Christian camp were disturbed by the new emphasis on man rather than God, and on the philosophy of the ancient - pagan - world.

Savonarola can be seen, in certain ways, as a mirror image of Machiavelli - a man who saw the incompatibility of classical and

Christian from within the Church. Indeed, at one point in *The Prince* Machiavelli borrows from Savonarola word-for-word, except that he turns the friar's condemnations into his commendations. But, as we saw in Chapter five in relation to the bonfire of vanities, Savonarola was no anti-intellectual barbarian. His friary of S. Marco had been rebuilt by Cosimo de' Medici and endowed with a rich store of books, including many Greek and Latin manuscripts. When the Medici fell from power in 1494, Savonarola ensured that the Medici library was saved from pillage by incorporating it into the Library of S. Marco. When Savonarola was dominant in the city, leading humanist scholars became friars of S. Marco, as did Michelangelo's brother. Savonarola's relationship with the Florentine Neoplatonists was ambiguous. In debates with Pico della Mirandola, Savonarola condemned Plato and Aristotle with uncompromising rigour, but Marsiglio Ficino listened to some of his sermons with admiration and as Pico lay dying he took the Dominican habit from Savonarola's own hands. Many of the educated élite who sought to understand humankind, saw the truth as some unresolved amalgam of the classical and the Christian, but were uncomfortable with the anomalies that lay therein.

The painter Sandro Botticelli, who was nearing the end of his life when Savonarola became dominant in Florence, was one of the many who fell under his spell. This profound religious experience made him question whether the classical subject matter of his great allegorical pictures was appropriate for a Christian. For a while he abandoned painting altogether, then he produced a few deeply religious works in which the symbolism seems wholly spiritual. But his earlier work was far from being entirely pagan. Indeed, his great *Birth Of Venus* depicted the pagan goddess of love in a way which echoed the form of many contemporary paintings of the baptism of Christ. The naked god/goddess stands in the centre outlined by water, to the right of him/her is a figure with the right arm raised, as in the act of baptism while, on the left, two other figures observe the scene. Moreover, most of Botticelli's earlier works were on Christian themes, a point true of the subject matter of Renaissance paintings in general. Although the depiction of classical subjects increased significantly in the 50 years after the painting of the *Primavera*, Virgins continued to outnumber Venuses. Peter Burke has calculated that secular subjects constituted 5 per cent of dated paintings in the 1480s and 25 per cent in the 1530s.[2] The majority of paintings both in the Early and in the High Renaissance were religious in character. Christianity remained dominant in an age famed for its revival of the classical, but the conflict between the two was never satisfactorily resolved.

We said above that Michelangelo 'gloried in the ambiguities' of the meeting of the classical and Christian worlds. This was true of most, but not all, of the 73 years he was an active artist. As he approached death his emphasis became more exclusively Christian, but for most of his career he explored this critical encounter. In a small circular painting of the Holy Family commissioned by the Florentine merchant family, the Doni, he set the foreground figures of Jesus, Mary and Joseph in front of a row of classical, naked youths. A child, usually identified as St John the Baptist, links the two. St John was often used to symbolise the link between the Old Testament, and new promise of Christ, but here Michelangelo uses him to establish a similar link between classical and Christian. The same theme can be found in much of his greatest work. In the marbles *David* and *Moses* and most explicitly in his painting of the ceiling of the Sistine Chapel, Michelangelo sought to communicate his vision of humanity by juxtaposing the classical and the Christian, and in doing so he was building on a well established Renaissance tradition.

3 Renaissance Italy and the Italian Renaissance

The term Renaissance Italy denotes not only a period in time but also a geographical area. The Renaissance did not affect the whole of Italy in the same way, to the same degree or at the same time. Generally speaking, the Florentine Renaissance was earlier, the Venetian later. North and central Italy experienced a Renaissance which most of the south never knew. The Renaissance phenomenon never significantly leaked out of the towns into the countryside. So, by *Renaissance* Italy we mean Florence, Rome, Venice, Milan and perhaps 20 or 30 other towns; we might do well to refer to the rest of the country in this period as late medieval or early modern Italy. This implies that the Renaissance was more than just a label for a period in time; that it had distinctive characteristics. At the end of the third section of Chapter one, which you would do well to read again now, we noted that it was inappropriate to attempt to define the Renaissance before examining the evidence on which such a definition should be based. As you read Chapter one, you might have assumed such an undertaking would be easy; if you have read the intervening chapters carefully and thoughtfully, you will now realise how difficult a job it is.

Partly the problem is one which always faces historians when they try to generalise about a range of unique events - no point will be true for the whole area over the whole period. It would be easier, for example, to define the Renaissance in Florence in the 1490s, or Rome in the 1510s, or Venice in the 1530s - the problem is that each of those definitions would be different, and they would all differ from a picture of Florence in the 1420s. Partly the difficulty is that definitions of the Italian Renaissance tend to describe the times and places at which the Renaissance spirit was at its most intense, although those moments are, by their very nature, untypical. If this book chose to base its picture of the Renaissance on, say, late fourteenth-century Perugia, its readers would feel cheated because the riches of fifteenth-century Florence or sixteenth-century Rome were ignored. The historian seems fated to deliver either an untypical version or a watered-down one. Having now reduced the reader's expectations, we may proceed with caution.

We can recognise the Renaissance as being different from the medieval world which preceded it and the modern one which followed, so it must therefore have had some distinctive characteristics. The development of capitalism with its emphasis on money, investment and profit created the urban centres in which the Renaissance thrived. It was not simply that money made from trade, manufacturing and banking allowed rich patrons to fund the activities of scholars and artists, but also early capitalist enterprise created a climate of boldness, a willingness to take risks, and an exciting atmosphere of innovation. The larger family remained a constant factor which provided stability, but, at least in Tuscany, households became smaller and some argue that this allowed more scope for individuals to emerge. In some states republican communes asserted themselves more firmly and established a constitutional rule of law as opposed to the anarchy of great families; in others a single family emerged as *signori*. In both the state became more powerful, though in neither were the major families eclipsed. States, whether republics or princedoms, remained loose alliances of great families. But cities were more ordered than before, and the leading families were more likely to be commercial than noble. In both princedoms and republics, learning and the arts flourished; the precise form of government does not seem to have been critical to the development of a Renaissance culture.

That culture was based, first and foremost, on the study of Greek and Latin texts of the Ancient World by humanist scholars. These sought out documents, studied them and reproduced them, first as manuscripts and later in a printed form. Although the Church needed reforming, Christianity remained a powerful element in Renaissance society and much humanist activity took place under its patronage, although some churchmen were alarmed by the concentration of interest in the pagan. Inspired by ancient examples, scholars wrote histories of their city which sometimes acted as propaganda for a princely patron. Theoreticians in their studies evolved an ideal of Renaissance Man, a balanced and harmonious being, both soldier and scholar who - if not the mythical Universal Man - had a variety of talents. But few such creatures existed in the real world and the dream of an invincible man who combined arms and letters, was largely shattered by the French invasion of 1494.

The essence of the Renaissance was to be found in small clusters, pools of talent where men of remarkable ability and vision fed off each other. One such was Florence in the 1420s when Brunelleschi, Masaccio and Donatello achieved a major breakthrough in the visual arts, whilst Leonardo Bruni was the humanist chancellor of the city. Another was Florence in the early 1490s when Lorenzo dominated the state and Savonarola thundered prophecies from his pulpit,

Ficino worked on Plato, Botticelli painted and the young Michelangelo began to carve marble. A third was Rome during the pontificate of Julius II (1503-13) when Raphael and Michelangelo both worked within the Vatican and papal troops drove Machiavelli out of Florence into the exile in which he was to write *The Prince*. But each of these snapshots is an untypically rich distillation which distorts the larger picture. Each is synoptic - a general view of different aspects of life drawn together - and that sense of interaction is crucial to the concept of Renaissance. In his 'Life of Masaccio', Vasari reflected

1   The appearance of a man of outstanding creative talent is very often
    accompanied by that of another great artist at the same time and in the
    same part of the world so that the two can inspire and emulate each
    other. Besides bringing considerable advantages to the two rivals them-
5   selves, this phenomenon of nature provides tremendous inspiration for
    later artists ...[3]

What was most remarkable about Renaissance Italy was the coming together of a number of greatly talented men at the same time and in the same places so that they were able to inspire each other in their quest to understand the nature of mankind and of human society and to express that understanding in books of prose and poetry, in paintings, sculptures and architecture.

What then, in summary, was the Italian Renaissance? If it had been possible to encapsulate in a final paragraph or a concluding chapter the answer to that question, I would not have needed to write the rest of this book. The whole of the book is the briefest summary I am able to offer. If you want to know what the Renaissance was, then you must read all of this book and as many other books as you can. There is no royal road to learning.

4 Renaissance Italy and the Modern World

The purpose of history is to understand the past. Beware of those people who tell you that it explains the present and insist that they spell out to you in detail what they mean. Too often this claim is just an empty excuse which historians use to justify their own existence. Life in Renaissance Italy was essentially different from life today; it overvalued tradition and undervalued experience, it was élitist and hierarchical, obsessed with ritual and ceremony. Its study has no real relevance to life in the modern world - except in a profound and radical way.

As people are born into a society and socialised into a world, they are in danger of thinking that the way things *are* is, in some sense, natural and right. Hence, parliamentary democracy, subjective personal moralities, concern for animals, the environment and human rights, advertising and consumerism, and mass access to higher education are in danger of seeming natural to human beings, rather than one culturally learned set of options. A society with quite different values, like Renaissance Italy, can help to open our eyes to other possibilities. Human society can be organised in a whole variety of different ways and those people who tell you that there is no alternative to present-day arrangements should not be believed. The major 'relevance' of Renaissance Italy to the modern world is that it shows that humankind can order itself and view the world in fundamentally different ways to those into which we are now socialised.

Renaissance Italy has little or no connection with the short-lived, superficial details of life in the present day. Yet Renaissance people thought deeply about the nature of humanity and the purpose of life and, although we shall probably reach very different conclusions from theirs, we must face the same questions and may be inspired by their search. The way in which you and I respond to a painting of Masaccio or a sculpture of Michelangelo and seek to resolve the profound human questions posed in it, can be the point at which the Renaissance and the modern world intersect.

References

1 Aristotle, *Politics* (Dent, 1959), p. 7.
2 Burke, *Renaissance Italy*, p. 279.
3 Vasari, *Lives of the Artists*, vol. 1, p. 124.

Summary Diagram
Conclusion

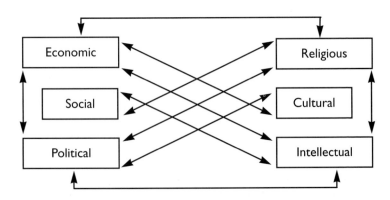

Answering essay questions on 'Renaissance Italy'

1. Why was there a Renaissance of the arts in fifteenth-century Italy?
2. What were the main characteristics of Italy between the late-fourteenth century and the early-sixteenth century which have led to it being described as a period of 'Renaissance'?
3. 'Renaissance Italy used the legacy of the Ancient World to help create something new.' Discuss.
4. How did the Renaissance in Italy differ from the late middle ages?
5. How does a knowledge of the economic, social, political and religious history of Italy in the fifteenth century help you to understand the Renaissance in learning and the arts?

Chronological Table

1290s	Venetian *serràta* established the Patriciate
1309-78	Papacy resides at Avignon
1337	Death of Giotto
1348	Black Death
1374	Death of Petrarch
1375	Death of Boccaccio
1375-1406	Coluccio Salutati Chancellor of Florence
1378-1417	The Great Schism, with two or three rival popes
1378	Revolt of the Ciompi in Florence
1385-1402	Giangaleazzo Visconti, Duke of Milan
1397-1400	Manuel Chrysoloras Professor of Greek at Florence
1398	Manuel Chrysoloras's Greek Grammar
1401	Competition for Baptistery Doors design in Florence
1401	Leonardo Bruni's *Panegyric of the City of Florence*
1403-52	Poggio Bracciolini employed at the papal court
1408-43	Donatello active as sculptor in Florence
1409	General Council of the Church at Pisa
1412-47	Filippo Maria Visconti Duke of Milan
1414-18	General Council of the Church at Constance
1414-35	Giovanna II Queen of Naples
1414	Start of Turkish expansion in the eastern Mediterranean
1415	Donatello's *St George* for Orsanmichele
1417-31	Pontificate of Martin V
1418	Competition for Cathedral Dome design in Florence
1419	Brunelleschi starts work on the Innocenti Hospital
1420	Brunelleschi starts work on Florence Cathedral Dome
1424-28	Masaccio active painting in Florence: *Tribute Money*
1425	Establishment of the *Monte della dote* in Florence
1427-44	Leonardo Bruni Chancellor of Florence
1427	Tuscan Castato tax returns
1429-60	Guarino da Verona's grammar school at Ferrara
1431-47	Pontificate of Eugenius IV
1431-49	General Council of the Church at Basle
1434-64	Cosimo de' Medici leading citizen of Florence
1435-42	War of Neapolitan Succession
1437-45	General Council of the Church at Ferrara/Florence
1442-58	Alfonso I King of Naples
1447-50	Ambrosian Republic in Milan
1447-55	Pontificate of Nicholas V
1448	Flavio Biondo employed at the court of Naples
1450-66	Francesco Sforza Duke of Milan
1450	Giovanni Simonetta employed at the court of Milan
1453	Fall of Constantinople
1457	Deposition of Francesco Foscari as Doge of Venice
1458-64	Pontificate of Pius II
1458-94	Ferrante I King of Naples

1458	Council of 100 (the *Cento*) established in Florence
1462-69	Marsiglio Ficino translated Plato's dialogues
1469-74	Marsiglio Ficino wrote his *Theologica Platonica*
1469-92	Lorenzo de' Medici leading citizen of Florence
1470-92	Botticelli active as painter in Florence
1474	Federigo da Montefeltro created Duke of Urbino
1478	Giuliano de' Medici assassinated in Pazzi Conspiracy
1480	Council of 70 established in Florence
1484	Marsiglio Ficino's translation of Plato published
1486	Pico della Mirandola publishes his 900 theses
1491	Savonarola becomes Prior of S. Marco, Florence
1492-1503	Pontificate of Alexander VI (Rodrigo Borgia)
1492-94	Piero de' Medici leading citizen of Florence
1494-1500	Lodovico *Il Moro* Sforza Duke of Milan
1494	French Invasion of Italy
1495	Charles VIII of France enters Naples
1497	Savonarola's first 'bonfire of vanities' in Florence
1498	Savonarola hanged and his body burned in Florence
1498-1512	Machiavelli bureaucrat for the Florentine Republic
1501-04	Michelangelo's marble *David* in Florence
1502-06	Leonardo active as painter in Florence
1502	Piero Soderini made *Gonfalonier* for life in Florence
1503-13	Pontificate of Julius II
1504-08	Raphael active as painter in Florence
1505	Machiavelli establishes a Florentine militia
1506-13	Leonardo active as painter in Milan
1508-12	Michelangelo painting ceiling of Sistine Chapel
1508-20	Raphael active as painter in Rome
1508-28	Castiglione writes *The Book of the Courtier*
1511	Raphael's *School of Athens* in the Vatican finished
1512	Restoration of a Medici regime in Florence
1513	Machiavelli's *The Prince*
1513-19	Machiavelli's *The Discourses on Livy*
1513-21	Pontificate of Leo X (Giovanni de' Medici)
1516	Venetian Jews confined in the ghetto
1523-34	Pontificate of Clement VII (Giulio de' Medici)
1527	Sack of Rome by Imperial Armies
1536-41	Michelangelo painting altar wall of Sistine Chapel
1537-40	Francesco Guicciardini's *Storia d'Italia*
1537	The Medici become the dukes of Florence
1545-63	Council of Trent reforms the Catholic Church
1564	Death of Michelangelo

Further Reading

Students of the Italian Renaissance are lucky to have many primary sources available in English translation. Penguin Classics publish important individual works by Machiavelli, Castiglione, Alberti, Vasari and others, but the following collections may give you wider scope. *The Portable Renaissance Reader* (Penguin, 1977) places Italy in the European context, whilst G. Brucker (ed.), *The Society of Renaissance Florence: a documentary study* (Harper and Row, 1971) and D. Chambers and B. Pullan (eds), *Venice: A Documentary History 1450-1630* (Blackwell, 1992) provide rich insights into major cities. J.R. Hale, *The Civilization of Europe in the Renaissance* (Collins, 1993) sets the Italian experience in a continental frame. Students are less well served by introductory surveys which cover the entire Italian peninsula over the full period. Denys Hay and John Law, *Italy in the Age of the Renaissance 1380-1530* (Longman, 1989) is excellent on the south and the islands, but, in redressing the balance, rather neglects the main centres. Students are recommended to concentrate on studies of individual cities and specific themes.

On Florence, Gene Brucker, *Renaissance Florence* (Wiley, 1969) and John Hale, *Florence and the Medici: The Pattern of Control* (Thames and Hudson, 1977) provide brilliant and highly readable introductions. Richard Trexler, *Public Life in Renaissance Florence* (Cornell UP, 1980) offers an important reinterpretation. F.A. Lewes, *Cosimo 'Il Vecchio' de' Medici, 1389-1464* (OUP, 1992) collects together a range of important articles on the first great Medici. Judith Hook, *Lorenzo de' Medici* (Hamilton, 1984) is the best biography of his grandson. N. Rubinstein, *The Government of Florence under the Medici 1434-1494* (OUP, 1966) remains the authoritative account.

On Venice, D.S. Chambers, *The Imperial Age of Venice 1380-1580* (Thames and Hudson, 1970) is still the best introduction. R. Finlay, *Politics in Renaissance Venice* (Benn, 1980) and B. Pullan, *Rich and Poor in Renaissance Venice* (Blackwell, 1971) give excellent treatments of political and social affairs respectively. F. C. Lane, *Venice: A Maritime Republic* (John Hopkins University Press, 1973) and J.J. Norwich, *A History of Venice* (Penguin Books, 1983) provide extensive narrative accounts. Sex and violence in Renaissance Venice are given authoritative, scholarly and unsensational treatments in G. Ruggiero, *The Boundaries of Eros: Sex Crime and Sexuality in Renaissance Venice* (OUP, 1985) and G. Ruggiero, *Violence in Early Renaissance Venice* (Rutyers UP, 1980).

On the city of Rome, P. Partner, *Renaissance Rome 1500-1559: a portrait of a society* (University of California Press, 1977) and on the church, D. Hay, *The Church in Italy in the Fifteenth Century* (CUP, 1977) provide outstanding introductions. M. Mallett, *The Borgias* (Bodley Head, 1969) is both readable and definitive. C. Shaw, *Julius II: The Warrior Pope* (Blackwell, 1993) is a good recent biography.

On Renaissance Humanism, P.O. Kristeller, *Renaissance concepts of man* (Harper & Row, 1972) presents the classic interpretation. James Hankins, *Plato in the Italian Renaissance* (Brill, 1990) and N.G. Wilson, *From Byzantium to Italy: Greek studies in the Italian Renaissance* (Bristol Classical Press, 1992) reassess the importance of the Neoplatonists in Greek studies. Highly lucid accounts are provided by G. Holmes, *The Florentine Enlightenment 1400-50* (Weidenfeld and Nicholson, 1969) and P. Burke, *Tradition and Innovation in Renaissance Italy* (Fontana, 1974).

New books on Machiavelli appear every year, but S. Anglo, *Machiavelli: a dissection* (Gollancz, 1969) has yet to be bettered as an clear and thoughtful introduction. Q. Skinner, *Machiavelli* (OUP, 1981), places him firmly in his humanist background, and Bernard Crick's 'Introduction' to Machiavelli, *The Discourses* (Penguin Books, 1970) is a wide-ranging essay on the author, not just that specific work. Michael Mallett, *Mercenaries and their Masters: Warfare in Renaissance Italy* (Bodley Head, 1974) defends the mercenaries from their humanist critics, and David Abulafia (ed.), *The French Descent into Renaissance Italy, 1494-95: Antecedents and effects* (Variorum, 1995) collects together the best recent work on the invasion of 1494.

On the art business, M. Baxendall, *Painting and Experience in Fifteenth Century Italy* (OUP, 1972), is outstanding, scholarly and highly readable - personally, I have never read a more exciting book. A. Thomas, *The Painter's Practice in Renaissance Tuscany* (CUP, 1995) provides a detailed account of artists' workshops. The definitive account of the works of art themselves is F. Hartt, *A History of Italian Renaissance Art* (Thames and Hudson, 1980) but many of the volumes in the Thames and Hudson World of Art Library series provide more manageable introductions to specific periods or places and to individual artists.

Better than reading about paintings and sculptures is looking at them. Many provincial galleries (like the Walker Gallery in Liverpool) have some Renaissance paintings worth seeing, but it well repays the effort to get to London to visit The National Gallery, where you will see important paintings by Masaccio, Botticelli, Leonardo, Raphael and Michelangelo, and the Victoria and Albert Museum, where works by Donatello and Raphael are on show. Do not try to see too much in one visit; limit yourself to a few works and spent at least 15 minutes looking at each. In the Victoria and Albert Museum, as well as the original works of art, the Cast Court has 'life-size', three-dimensional reproductions of the major pieces of Renaissance sculpture. This is rather like looking at photographs of a painting and, although useful if you cannot get to Italy, it is no substitute for the real things. So get to the Louvre in Paris, if you can, for major painting and sculpture. Even better, go to Florence for the Uffizi, the Bargello and the Accademia, and to Rome for the Vatican palace and the Sistine Chapel. It is not as far as you may think.

Index

Acknowledgements

The publishers would like to thank the following for their permission to use copyright illustrations:

Robert Hole pp 27, 102; AKG Photo, London the front cover, pp 63, 85, 113, 115, 117; The Bridgeman Art Library, London pp 110, 119; Corbis p 105.

The author and publishers would like to thank the following for permission to use material in this volume:

Allen & Unwin for the extract from *Memoirs of a Renaissance Pope: The Commentaries of Pius II* by L.C. Gabel (ed.) (1959); Benn for the extract from *Politics in Renaissance Venice* by R. Finlay (1980); Blackwell for the extracts from *Venice: A Documentary History 1450-1630* by D. Chambers and B. Pullen (eds) (1992); Bodley Head for the extract from *The Borgias: The Rise and Fall of a Renaissance Dynasty* by Michael Mallet (1969); Columbia University Press for the extract from *Plato in the Italian Renaissance Vol. One* by James Hawkins (1990); Dover Publications for the extract from *The Craftsman's Handbook* by Cennini (1933/1960); Harper & Row for the extracts from *The Society of Renaissance Florence: a documentary study* by G. Brucker (ed.) (1971), and *Renaissance Princes, Popes, and Prelates* by Vespasiano (1963); Macmillan for the extracts from *The History of Italy* by F. Guicciardini (1969), and *Patrons and Artists in the Italian Renaissance* by Chambers (1970); Oxford University Press for the extracts from *The Literary Works of Machiavelli* by J.R. Hale (ed.) (1961); Penguin Books for extracts from *The Discourses* by Machiavelli (1970 edition), *The Lives of the Artists* Vol. 1 by Vasari (1965 edition), *The Prince* by Machiavelli (1961 edition), *On Painting* [1435] by Leon Battista Alberti (1991 edition), *The Courtier* by Castiglione (1967 edition), and *The Portable Renaissance Reader* by J.B. Ross and M.M. McLaughlin (eds.) (1977); Princeton University Press for the extract from *The Crisis of the Early Italian Renaissance* by H. Baron (1995); the extract adapted from *The French Descent into Renaissance Italy, 1494-95: Antecedents and Effects* edited by David Abulafia, Variorum 1995, Ashgate Publishing Ltd; and Vintage Books for the extract from *Complete Poems and Selected Letters* by Michelangelo (1970).

Every effort has been made to trace and acknowledge ownership of copyright. The publishers will be glad to make suitable arrangements with any copyright holders whom it has not been possible to contact.